SOUTH PENNINE WALKS

AN ILLUSTRATED GUIDE TO
THIRTY CIRCULAR WALKS
OF OUTSTANDING BEAUTY AND INTEREST

JACK KEIGHLEY

i

LYCH GATE
WORSTHORNE CHURCH

WALK II

SOUTH PENNINE WALKS

☆

AN ILLUSTRATED GUIDE TO THIRTY CIRCULAR WALKS OF OUTSTANDING BEAUTY AND INTEREST

by

Ffrei Ghley

CICERONE

2 POLICE SQUARE, MILNTHORPE, CUMBRIA LA7 7PY
www.cicerone.co.uk

ISBN 1 85284 390 X

Also by 𝒥Keighley

WALKS IN THE YORKSHIRE DALES
ISBN 1 85284 054 X

WALKS IN THE YORKSHIRE DALES BOOK TWO
ISBN 1 85284 065 X

WALKS IN THE YORKSHIRE DALES BOOK THREE
ISBN 1 85284 085 4

WALKS IN LANCASHIRE WITCH COUNTRY
ISBN 1 85284 093 5

WALKS ON THE NORTH YORK MOORS
ISBN 1 85284 134 6

WALKS ON THE NORTH YORK MOORS BOOK TWO
ISBN 1 85284 197 4

FAMILY WALKS IN THE FOREST OF BOWLAND
ISBN 1 85284 251 2

WALKS IN RIBBLE COUNTRY
ISBN 1 85284 284 9

WALKS IN DALES COUNTRY
ISBN 1 85284 323 3

INTRODUCTION

For the purposes of this guidebook, the term 'South Pennines' is taken to refer to the expanse of hill country which straddles the Lancashire/Yorkshire border 'twixt the Yorkshire Dales and Peak National Parks. Though standing virtually 'on the doorstep' for millions of people, it tends to be overshadowed, from a recreational point of view, by the aforementioned National Parks, which attract hordes of visitors whilst the wild moors, dark, dramatic crags and beautiful wooded valleys of the South Pennines remain relatively neglected.

The Pennine ridge was formed by a great upheaval, or anticline, of rocks which had been laid down some 280 million years ago, when the area was a vast river delta. The Pennine anticline is thought to have risen to a height of well over 10,000 feet, but during the ensuing aeons the softer rocks, such as shale and limestone, have been slowly eroded from its top to leave a surface of the harder, more weather-resistant millstone grit. Into this the glaciers and meltwaters of the Ice Ages have gouged the deep valleys, or cloughs, which are such a distinctive feature of the region.

Though nature has lavishly provided some splendid scenery, it is the human hand which has been largely instrumental in creating today's unique South Pennine landscape. Man's need of farmland and timber led to the destruction of the dense woodland which clothed much of the area in medieval times, and constant grazing by livestock has prevented regeneration. In the later Middle Ages small-scale woollen industries began to develop, and in remote, crag-fringed cloughs you will find the crumbling ruins of once-thriving mills whose waterwheels were driven by rushing streams until the advent of steam-power took the industry down into the main valleys.

The entire South Pennine region is crisscrossed by a vast and intricate network of footpaths. Some are old byways once used by miners and millworkers, others are ancient roads, and many are trading routes trodden in the 17th and 18th centuries by plodding teams of packhorses heavily laden with such commodities as salt, lime, coal and cloth. The coming of canals and railways spelt the end of the packhorse era, but the old paths, with their numerous sections of ancient stone causeways, remain in use as delightful walkers' routes.

Millstone grit is an impervious rock, and thus the moors tend to be boggy, but they DO make excellent water-catchment areas, and many reservoirs have been built to take advantage of this. In a region devoid of natural lakes these reservoirs attract wildlife and often add beauty and interest to what might otherwise be featureless terrain. Countless disused quarries reveal where stone has been obtained for building the massive reservoir dams, mullion-windowed farmhouses and the now smoke-blackened old mills and weavers' cottages.

There is no doubt that the true flavour of the South Pennines lies in its unique amalgamation of town and country, mills and hills. Wild, desolate moors, rugged cliffs and outcrops, richly-wooded cloughs, flowery meadows, 'time-warp' villages and fascinating industrial relics all intermingle to fashion a landscape of quite spectacular contrasts. Incredibly varied walking experiences are here on free offer - get out and sample some NOW.

Keighley

November 2002

SOME WORDS OF ADVICE

● Many of the routes in this book cross agricultural land, and farmers will not welcome inconsiderate visitors. When crossing fields keep closely to paths and walk in single file across meadowland. Avoid climbing walls, and securely close all gates behind you (unless they are obviously meant to be left open).

● Leave no litter.

● Cars must not be parked where they obstruct field gates or cause damage to grass verges. Lock your car and hide from view any attractive or valuable articles (or take them with you).

● Most of the walks described in this book cross high, exposed moorland terrain where the weather conditions may be less pleasant than at valley level. Should the weather turn nasty, don't hesitate to call it a day and return by the route along which you came.

● Before setting out, let others know exactly where you're going (especially if you're walking alone).

● When walking along a motor-road walk on the RIGHT to face oncoming traffic. The exception to this is on approaching a blind right-hand bend, when you should cross to the left for a clearer view.

 CLOTHING AND EQUIPMENT Boots or strong, comfortable shoes are essential (on the high moors and in winter BOOTS are the ONLY appropriate footwear). A windproof jacket (preferably with a hood) will be needed. Thick, heavy sweaters are not recommended — two or three lightweight layers are warmer and more adaptable to changing conditions. Denim is not at all suitable. In cold weather a woollen hat or cap will prevent the loss of a great deal of body heat. A rucsac is necessary. A small 'daysac' with a capacity of about 20 – 25 litres would be adequate for any of these walks. The author's rucsac will always contain the following items : –
● waterproof jacket and overtrousers ● small first-aid kit ● spare laces ● large-scale O.S. map ● compass ● plastic bottle for cold drink and/or flask for coffee or soup ● whistle ● high-calorie snack (e.g. chocolate or crisps) ● dog's drinking-water in a plastic bottle with either a 'cup top' or a separate small bowl.

In very wet, muddy conditions gaiters are an asset, once you've managed to get them on (it helps if you're a contortionist). A walking-stick is a matter of personal preference. Some walkers wouldn't be seen dead with one, but the author finds a knobstick useful for steep, slippery descents, fording streams, beating down nettles, discouraging aggressive animals and testing potentially boggy ground prior to sinking in up to the knees.

6

CHILDREN

When taking children on country walks some thought must be given to the distance and the type of terrain involved. Until you're sure of the child's capabilities, keep the distances short. Most of the walks in this book would probably be too much for a child under the age of five. As a rough rule-of-thumb, a child should be able to manage about a mile for each year of his age after his fifth birthday. Children should be warmly clothed and well shod. One cannot always afford to buy expensive boots for growing feet, but at least the child should have strong shoes or close-fitting wellingtons. Under no circumstances should young children be allowed to wander off beyond the range of vision of responsible adults, and extreme care and control must be exercised in the vicinity of crags, old mine-workings, quarries and motor-roads.

DOGS

Though dogs are generally better-behaved than children they can nevertheless present certain difficulties which the owner should bear in mind. The two main problems are livestock and stiles — particularly ladder-stiles. Dogs should be kept under close control at all times, and MUST be on a lead in the proximity of farms and farm livestock. A lead should also be used when walking on motor-roads or on moorland during nesting-time (April-June). Some large, agile dogs are able to scramble over ladder-stiles, but small models need to be lifted over, and this can sometimes be awkward if you're walking alone. If your dog is big, fat and rheumaticky then you have problems. Best places for dogs are high, open ground and woodland ; worst are motor-roads and lowland pastures. On very hot, sunny days dogs can become distressed and may be at risk of heat-stroke. On summer walks the author has in his rucsac a small, plastic spray-bottle of water.

PLEASE OBSERVE THE COUNTRY CODE

- Keep to public paths across farmland
- Fasten all gates
- Leave no litter
- Make no unnecessary noise
- Keep your dog under close control
- Protect wildlife, plants and trees
- Leave livestock, crops and machinery alone
- Enjoy the countryside and respect its life and work
- Help to keep all water clean
- Guard against all risk of fire
- Take special care on country roads
- Use gates and stiles to cross walls and fences

THE WALKS

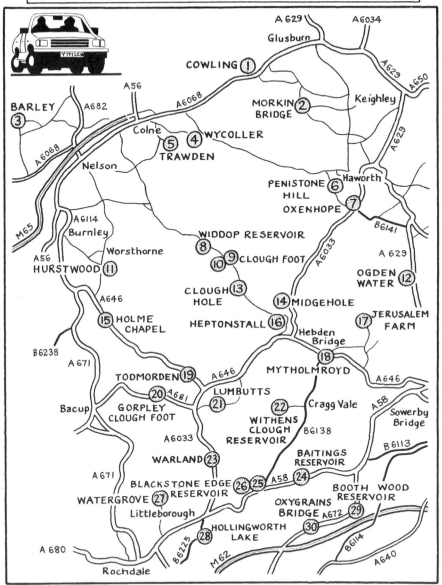

ALL THESE WALKS CAN BE FOUND ON THE
ORDNANCE SURVEY 1:25 000 MAP OF THE
SOUTH PENNINES (OUTDOOR LEISURE 21).

ABOUT THIS BOOK

All the walks described in this book are circular, and begin at a place where a car may be parked without causing an obstruction. They are fairly uniform in length, an average of about 6 miles making them half-day rather than full-day excursions. The routes, which adhere to public rights-of-way and permissive paths, should be free from serious difficulty and well within the capability of reasonably fit and agile walkers. Although the author has personally researched and walked all these routes, it must be pointed out that changes will occur quite frequently. Walkers may expect to encounter new stiles and fences and sometimes even diversions — either temporary or permanent. In such cases please note and obey all legitimate waymarks and signs.

NEITHER THE AUTHOR NOR THE PUBLISHER CAN ACCEPT RESPONSIBILITY FOR ANY ACCIDENT OR MISADVENTURE INCURRED ON THESE WALKS.

THE MAPS

The strip-maps show all relevant route-finding features, and great care has been taken to ensure accuracy, although for the sake of clarity there is deliberate distortion of scale in depicting routes along, for example, narrow lanes or through farmyards. In all maps north is at the top. In the ROUTE DIRECTIONS any mention of a stile, gate or footbridge means that it is used, unless otherwise stated. The maps and route directions together should suffice to make it quite clear to you how you've got lost. It is, however, strongly recommended that an Ordnance Survey map be carried, as this will add interest and enable the walker to identify distant features not mentioned in the text.

SYMBOLS USED ON THE MAPS

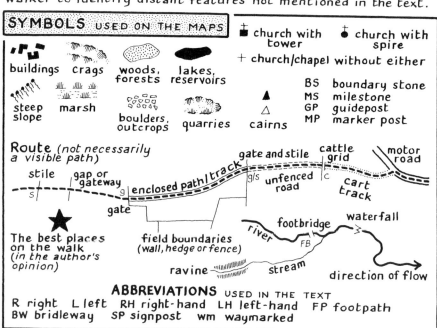

buildings   crags   woods, forests   lakes, reservoirs

steep slope   marsh   boulders, outcrops   quarries   cairns

‡ church with tower   ● church with spire
+ church/chapel without either

BS   boundary stone
MS   milestone
GP   guidepost
MP   marker post

Route (not necessarily a visible path)

stile   gap or gateway   enclosed path/track   gate and stile   cattle grid   motor road

g/s unfenced road   c   cart track   gate

★ The best places on the walk (in the author's opinion)

field boundaries (wall, hedge or fence)

river   footbridge   FB   waterfall

ravine   stream   direction of flow

ABBREVIATIONS USED IN THE TEXT
R right   L left   RH right-hand   LH left-hand   FP footpath
BW bridleway   SP signpost   wm waymarked

TOURIST INFORMATION CENTRES

BRADFORD Central Library Prince's Way
Tel : 01274 753678

BURNLEY Burnley Mechanics Manchester Road
Tel : 01282 664421

HALIFAX Piece Hall Tel : 01422 368725

HAWORTH 2-4 West Lane Tel : 01535 642329

HEBDEN BRIDGE 1 Bridge Gate Tel : 01422 843831

KEIGHLEY Town Hall Bow Street Tel : 01535 618014

RAWTENSTALL 41-45 Kay Street Tel : 01706 226590

ROCHDALE The Clock Tower Town Hall Tel : 01706 356592

TODMORDEN 15 Burnley Road Tel : 01706 818181

COUNTRYSIDE & HERITAGE CENTRES

HOLLINGWORTH LAKE COUNTRY PARK
Littleborough Tel : 01706 373421

OGDEN WATER COUNTRYSIDE CENTRE
Ovenden Halifax Tel : 01422 249136

PENDLE HERITAGE CENTRE
Park Hill Barrowford Tel : 01282 695366

THE COACH HOUSE Littleborough Tel : 01706 378481

USEFUL ADDRESSES

THE RAMBLERS' ASSOCIATION 1-5 Wandsworth Road
London SW8 2XX Tel : 0171 582 6878

CALDERDALE COUNTRYSIDE SERVICE Leisure Services
Dept. Wellesley Park Halifax HX2 0AY Tel : 01422 359454

NATIONAL TRUST (Regional Office) 27 Tadcaster Road
York YO2 2QG Tel : 01904 702021

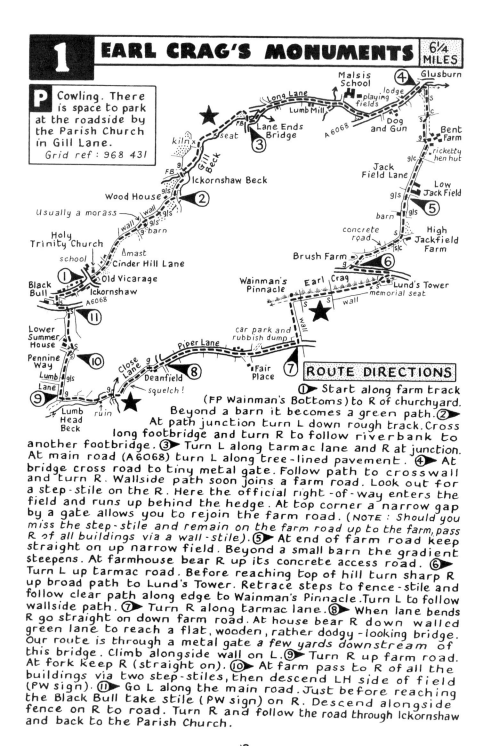

1 EARL CRAG'S MONUMENTS 6¼ MILES

P Cowling. There is space to park at the roadside by the Parish Church in Gill Lane.
Grid ref : 968 431

Malsis School · Glusburn ④
lodge · playing fields
Long Lane · Lumb Mill
Lane Ends Bridge ③
seat · FB · kiln
A 6068 · Dog and Gun
Bent Farm
ricketty hen hut
Gill Beck · FB
Ickornshaw Beck · Jack Field Lane
Wood House ② · Low Jack Field
Usually a morass · wall · gls · barn · barn ⑤
Holy Trinity Church · concrete road · High Jackfield Farm
school · mast · Cinder Hill Lane
Brush Farm ⑥
Old Vicarage · Wainman's Pinnacle · Earl Crag · Lund's Tower
Black Bull ① · Ickornshaw · memorial seat
A6068 · wall
⑪ · ★ · wall
Lower Summer House · car park and rubbish dump
Pennine Way · Piper Lane · Fair Place ⑦
Lumb Lane ⑩ · Close Lane · squelch! · Deanfield ⑧
⑨ · ruin · Lumb Head Beck

ROUTE DIRECTIONS

①▶ Start along farm track (FP Wainman's Bottoms) to R of churchyard. Beyond a barn it becomes a green path. ②▶ At path junction turn L down rough track. Cross long footbridge and turn R to follow riverbank to another footbridge. ③▶ Turn L along tarmac lane and R at junction. At main road (A6068) turn L along tree-lined pavement. ④▶ At bridge cross road to tiny metal gate. Follow path to crosswall and turn R. Wallside path soon joins a farm road. Look out for a step-stile on the R. Here the official right-of-way enters the field and runs up behind the hedge. At top corner a narrow gap by a gate allows you to rejoin the farm road. (NOTE : Should you miss the step-stile and remain on the farm road up to the farm, pass R of all buildings via a wall -stile). ⑤▶ At end of farm road keep straight on up narrow field. Beyond a small barn the gradient steepens. At farmhouse bear R up its concrete access road. ⑥▶ Turn L up tarmac road. Before reaching top of hill turn sharp R up broad path to Lund's Tower. Retrace steps to fence-stile and follow clear path along edge to Wainman's Pinnacle. Turn L to follow wallside path. ⑦▶ Turn R along tarmac lane. ⑧▶ When lane bends R go straight on down farm road. At house bear R down walled green lane to reach a flat, wooden, rather dodgy-looking bridge. Our route is through a metal gate a few yards downstream of this bridge. Climb alongside wall on L. ⑨▶ Turn R up farm road. At fork keep R (straight on). ⑩▶ At farm pass to R of all the buildings via two step-stiles, then descend LH side of field (PW sign). ⑪▶ Go L along the main road. Just before reaching the Black Bull take stile (PW sign) on R. Descend alongside fence on R to road. Turn R and follow the road through Ickornshaw and back to the Parish Church.

MODERATELY STRENUOUS. A LOVELY RIVERSIDE STROLL PRECEDES A LONG AND EVER-STEEPENING CLIMB OF SOME 800' FROM GLUSBURN BRIDGE TO LUND'S TOWER, FROM WHERE THE EXHILARATING WALK TO WAINMAN'S PINNACLE IS ATOP A SUPERB GRITSTONE EDGE COMMANDING BREATHTAKING VIEWS OF SOUTH CRAVEN. AFTER SKIRTING THE SOMBRE WASTELANDS OF ICKORNSHAW MOOR, THE EASY-TO-FOLLOW ROUTE JOINS THE FAMOUS PENNINE WAY FOR A GENTLE CONCLUDING DESCENT. NO LADDER-STILES, BUT A COUPLE OF HIGH, AWKWARD STEP-STILES BETWEEN THE TWO MONUMENTS. 1½ MILES ON QUIET MOTOR-ROADS + 500 YARDS ALONG THE BUSY A6068 WHICH, FORTUNATELY, HAS A SEPARATE WALKWAY. TWO EXCELLENT PUBS EN ROUTE.

COWLING

The parish of Holy Trinity includes the two adjoining villages of Cowling and Ickornshaw. Cowling is much the larger of the two, and consists predominantly of gritstone terraced houses and factories strung out along the main Colne-Keighley road. Ickornshaw lies in a sheltered valley and is by contrast more rural in character, with pretty stone cottages clustered around a little stream. The rustic charm of the place is, however, badly marred by the huge Wesleyan chapel (1875), which is now a gaunt and derelict shell and appears to be in a dangerous condition. Close to the 19th C Parish Church stands the house which was the humble birthplace of Cowling's most famous son. Lord Philip Snowden, whose father was a local weaver, became the country's very first Labour Chancellor of the Exchequer in the government of Ramsay Macdonald (1924).

Lund's Tower — Wainman's Pinnacle

kiln near Gill Beck

LUND'S TOWER is a castellated edifice constructed by James Lund of Malsis Hall. Opinion varies as to whether he built it to celebrate the birth of his daughter Ethel or the Golden Jubilee of Queen Victoria (1887). The tower, which is also known as 'Sutton Pinnacle', 'Jubilee Tower' and 'Ethel's Tower', has an interior spiral staircase of 39 steps leading up to a viewing platform.

WAINMAN'S PINNACLE, or 'Cowling Pinnacle', also has a disputed origin. Some claim that a certain Lady Amcotts had it erected in memory of her husband, one of the Wainman family, who was killed at war. Others insist that it was built by Richard Wainman, either to mark the Battle of Waterloo (1815) or as a memorial to his son, who was killed in the Napoleonic War.

THE HITCHING STONE

Whilst plodding along Piper Lane, be sure to look L across Ickornshaw Moor to see a huge boulder on the skyline. This gigantic cube of gritstone is estimated to weigh around 1,000 tons, and is considered to be the largest detached boulder in Yorkshire. According to legend it originally stood on Rombald's Moor, in front of a witch's house. One day this old crone, in a violent fit of rage, grabbed her broomstick and flicked — or 'hitched'— the boulder across the valley to its present resting-place.

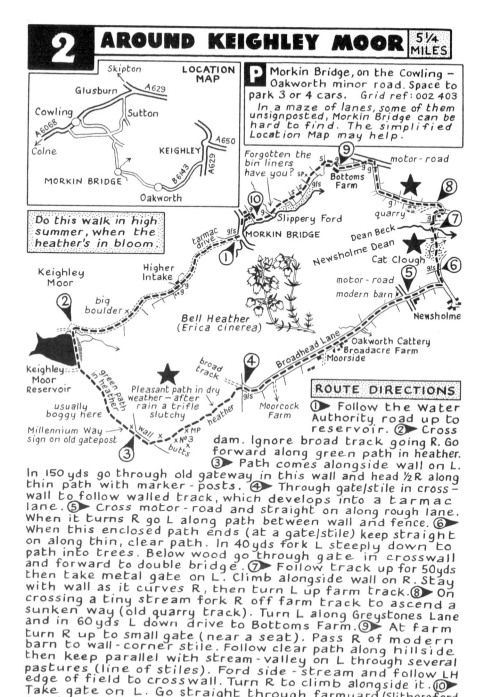

LOCATION MAP

Skipton · A629 · Glusburn · Sutton · Cowling · A6068 · Colne · MORKIN BRIDGE · Oakworth · KEIGHLEY · B6143 · A629 · A650

P Morkin Bridge, on the Cowling – Oakworth minor road. Space to park 3 or 4 cars. Grid ref: 002 403
In a maze of lanes, some of them unsignposted, Morkin Bridge can be hard to find. The simplified Location Map may help.

Do this walk in high summer, when the heather's in bloom.

motor-road · Forgotten the bin liners have you? · Bottoms Farm · ⑨ · ⑧ · quarry · ⑩ · Slippery Ford · ⑦ · MORKIN BRIDGE · Dean Beck · ① · tarmac drive · Newsholme Dean · Cat Clough · ⑥ · Higher Intake · Keighley Moor · ② · big boulder · motor-road · modern barn · ⑤ · Newsholme · Bell Heather (Erica cinerea) · Oakworth Cattery · Broadacre Farm · Moorside · Broadhead Lane · Keighley Moor Reservoir · green path in heather · broad track · ④ · usually boggy here · Pleasant path in dry weather – after rain a trifle slutchy · heather · Moorcock Farm · Millennium Way sign on old gatepost · ③ · wall · MP · No 3 · butts

ROUTE DIRECTIONS

①► Follow the water Authority road up to reservoir. ②► Cross broad track going R. Go forward along green path in heather. ③► Path comes alongside wall on L. In 150 yds go through old gateway in this wall and head ½R along thin path with marker-posts. ④► Through gate/stile in cross-wall to follow walled track, which develops into a tarmac lane. ⑤► Cross motor-road and straight on along rough lane. When it turns R go L along path between wall and fence. ⑥► When this enclosed path ends (at a gate/stile) keep straight on along thin, clear path. In 40 yds fork L steeply down to path into trees. Below wood go through gate in crosswall and forward to double bridge. ⑦► Follow track up for 50 yds then take metal gate on L. Climb alongside wall on R. Stay with wall as it curves R, then turn L up farm track. ⑧► On crossing a tiny stream fork R off farm track to ascend a sunken way (old quarry track). Turn L along Greystones Lane and in 60 yds L down drive to Bottoms Farm. ⑨► At farm turn R up to small gate (near a seat). Pass R of modern barn to wall-corner stile. Follow clear path along hillside then keep parallel with stream-valley on L through several pastures (line of stiles). Ford side-stream and follow LH edge of field to crosswall. Turn R to climb alongside it. ⑩► Take gate on L. Go straight through farmyard (Slitheroford Farm) and L down road to Morkin Bridge.

2

IN SOCCER PARLANCE MOST DEFINITELY A WALK OF TWO HALVES. AS FAR AS POINT ④ IT'S ALL WILD, WINDSWEPT MOORLAND, WHILST BEYOND POINT ⑥ WE FIND OURSELVES IN A VALLEY OF THE MOST EXQUISITE, SYLVAN BEAUTY. THE HALF-TIME INTERVAL, SO TO SPEAK, IS A RATHER DULL TRUDGE ALONG A STRAIGHT, WALLED LANE (BROADHEAD LANE). THE MOORLAND SECTION IS VERY EASY GOING, ALBEIT A LITTLE BOGGY IN PLACES (NOTHING SERIOUS). THE VALLEY SECTION IS SLIGHTLY MORE STRENUOUS. NO LADDER-STILES. MOTOR-ROAD WALKING NEGLIGIBLE.

! WARNING NEAR THE END OF THE WALK A STREAM MUST BE FORDED, WHICH AFTER RAIN MAY INVOLVE WADING THROUGH WATER ALMOST KNEE-DEEP. WHEN STARTING OUT ON THIS WALK, THE AUTHOR (BEING A SAGACIOUS FELLOW) WILL HAVE IN HIS RUCKSACK A COUPLE OF PLASTIC BIN-LINERS.

KEIGHLEY MOOR RESERVOIR

was built to serve local mills. Completed in 1846, it has a surface area of 17 acres. It is generally of bleak and dismal aspect, though it probably looks O.K. on a sunny day (the author has never visited it in other than atrocious weather). ★

NEWSHOLME

, which may be visited by making a short detour, is a 'dead-end' hamlet in that it has no through motor-road. Here you will find St. John's Chapel, a small church — possibly of 17th C. vintage — which is joined onto a farm.

This old red telephone box and Victorian postbox stand, along with various other curios and bits of bric-a-brac, at the entrance to Broadacre Farm.

The bizarre clapper bridge at point ⑦. A delightful place for a picnic.

HEATHER AND THE RED GROUSE

The red grouse, Britain's only indigenous bird, is dependent upon heather, which gives protection from harsh weather and predators as well as providing more than 75% of its dietary needs. The 'sport' of grouse-shooting became fashionable in the 1850s, following the invention of the breech-loading shotgun.

Landowners began to invest a lot of money in their moorland, and established a system of grouse-husbandry. Sheep were excluded, predators such as foxes and hawks were exterminated, and areas of heather were burned on a rotational basis to create a patchwork of different-aged growth for feeding, roosting and nesting.

Grouse butt Nº 3

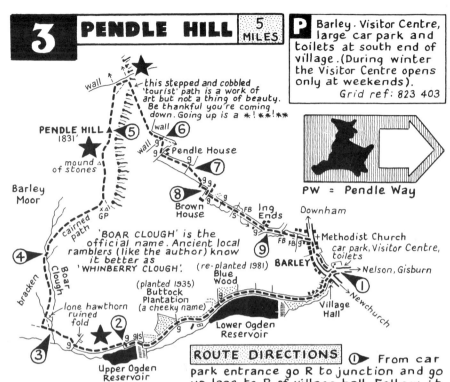

3 PENDLE HILL — 5 MILES

P Barley. Visitor Centre, large car park and toilets at south end of village.(During winter the Visitor Centre opens only at weekends).

Grid ref: 823 403

PW = Pendle Way

*this stepped and cobbled 'tourist' path is a work of art but not a thing of beauty. Be thankful you're coming down. Going up is a *!**!***

PENDLE HILL 1831'

mound of stones

wall (6)

wall (5)

g g Pendle House (7)

Barley Moor

cairned path GP

(4)

bracken

Boar Clough

g g (8)
Brown House

FB Ing Ends

Downham

+Methodist Church car park, Visitor Centre, toilets

'BOAR CLOUGH' is the official name. Ancient local ramblers (like the author) know it better as 'WHINBERRY CLOUGH'.

(re-planted 1981)

(9)

FB FB g

BARLEY

Nelson, Gisburn

Blue Wood

(planted 1935) Buttock Plantation (a cheeky name)

Village Hall

Newchurch

lone hawthorn ruined fold

(2)

(3)

g g g

Lower Ogden Reservoir

Upper Ogden Reservoir

ROUTE DIRECTIONS

① From car park entrance go R to junction and go up lane to R of village hall. Follow it past lower reservoir and on up the valley, ignoring two farm roads rising R, to a gate/stile below upper reservoir dam. Climb to R of dam and continue alongside reservoir between wall and fence.② Through swing-gate and continue alongside wall, which is now on your L. From gate in crosswall path rises steeply to R then levels out to reach Boar Clough (identified by its lone hawthorn).③ Cross small stream. Ignore path rising R. Pass L of wooden barrier and in about 100yds, at PW sign, turn sharp R up thin path which soon becomes broader as it climbs LH side of clough.④ Cross the stream and continue alongside it (wm). In about 200yds, at a cairn, path bears R, away from stream. Follow cairned path. It eventually swings L to join another path coming up from R. ⑤ At summit keep straight on (N) towards wall and ladder-stile. DON'T cross the stile, but turn R to descend by wall to guidestone and stile. DON'T cross this either, but turn R to descend 'constructed' path. ⑥ From gate below wall-corner fork R (FP Barley 1·8km) to gate at far side of buildings. Descend LH side of field to gate (wm). ⑦ In next field bear slightly R. Clear path develops in depression. Go through gate in wall and L down wall-side to another gate.⑧ Turn R along cart-track then L through swing-gate. Follow fence on L, ignoring a cattle-grid, to path on RH side of wall.⑨ Turn L along lane. Where lane bends L go R over footbridge, then turn L and,keeping parallel with stream, descend into village. Turn R along road. At Pendle Inn go through gap in wall on L and follow path to car park.

After the walk you may have time to visit the nearby village of Newchurch in Pendle, where there's a wonderfully spooky shop called 'WITCHES GALORE'. Adults will be bewitched and kids spellbound.

MODERATELY STRENUOUS, ALBEIT ONE OF THE EASIEST ROUTES UP PENDLE. 1075' OF ASCENT, THE HARDEST BIT BEING THE INITIAL STAGE OF THE CLIMB UP BOAR CLOUGH. THE LONG DESCENT OF THE STEEP, STEPPED, 'TOURIST' PATH CAN BE PRETTY KNEE-JARRING. NO LADDER-STILES. MOST OF THE GATES ARE OF THE 'SWING' OR 'KISSING' TYPE. MOTOR-ROAD WALKING NEGLIGIBLE. MAGNIFICENT VIEWS. EASY-TO-FOLLOW ROUTE IN NORMAL CONDITIONS, BUT PENDLE'S VAST UPPER SLOPES CAN BE VERY CONFUSING IN MIST.

3

Pendle Hill is somewhat isolated from the rest of the area covered by this book, and you may wonder how it merits inclusion. It qualifies on two counts :– a) It is generally regarded as an offshoot of the South Pennines. b) It's the author's favourite hill.

PENDLE HILL

dominates the surrounding countryside to a greater extent than does, perhaps, any other hill in the land. It is not a great mountain; in fact it is not a mountain at all, its summit failing by 169' to achieve that distinction. However, because of its isolated position – between the main S. Pennine Chain and the Bowland Fells – it rises majestically and appears much higher than it really is. What Pendle lacks in height it certainly makes up for in girth, being no less than seven miles long and covering an area of some twenty-five square miles. The top of the hill is a vast plateau of peat hags and coarse grasses, and the view must be one of the finest in England – a magnificent panorama. Legends of witchcraft and black magic, strange superstitions and whispered tales of supernatural happenings have given Pendle an almost mystical atmosphere. Pass close to the hill on a wild, drab winter's day and you half-expect to see a besom-mounted witch gliding silently by. The PENDLE WAY is a 45 mile circular walk around the Borough of Pendle, with waymarkers featuring a witch and yellow arrow.

BEWARE LOW FLYING WITCHES

A Pendle Way cairn

BARLEY

The size of the car park is an indication of the popularity of this small, attractive village with hikers and tourists. Barley dates back to the 13th C., when it was called 'Barelegh' (infertile lea or meadow). It has always been a farming community, but in Victorian times there were 2 cotton mills here. One of these, which we pass very early in the walk, was wrecked by floods in the 1880s and is now a Water Authority filter station.

OGDEN RESERVOIRS

The two reservoirs provide drinking water for the Nelson area. LOWER OGDEN RESERVOIR was completed in 1914. It has a surface area of 21·12 acres, a maximum depth of 59', and holds 157·5 million gallons. UPPER OGDEN RESERVOIR is older, being completed in 1906. It has an area of 7·01 acres, a maximum depth of 58', and a capacity of 54·5 million gallons. The illustration depicts the Lower Reservoir

Be sure to take a compass in case it's misty, and binoculars in case it's not.

For more – MUCH more – about PENDLE and the WITCHES, rush out NOW and buy WALKS IN LANCASHIRE WITCH COUNTRY (See P.4)

DOWNHAM

Guidepost at top of 'tourist' path

P Wycoller has two car parks – Haworth Road and Trawden Lane. Use the latter, reaching it by leaving the A6068 at either Colne or Laneshaw Bridge. Grid ref: 927 395

NOTE : Cars, save for those of residents, essential services and disabled badge holders, are not allowed to proceed beyond the car park.

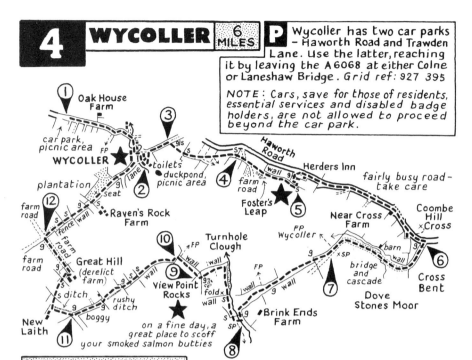

1 Oak House Farm

car park, picnic area FP
WYCOLLER ★
plantation
seat
farm road 12
Raven's Rock Farm
2
toilets, duckpond, picnic area
3
Haworth Road
Herders Inn
fairly busy road – take care
4 farm road
Foster's Leap 5
Near Cross Farm
Coombe Hill ×Cross
Great Hill (derelict farm)
9 View Point Rocks 10
Turnhole Clough
FP Wycoller
×SP
barn
bridge and cascade
6 Cross Bent
farm road
ditch
rushy ditch
boggy
fold×
wall st
FP
9 wall
7
Dove Stones Moor
New Laith 11
on a fine day, a great place to scoff your smoked salmon butties
Brink Ends Farm
SP
8

ROUTE DIRECTIONS

①► From car park go R down walkway, then lane, into village. ②► At far end of village go between Aisled Barn and toilets to path slanting L uphill. It soon turns R through wide gateway. ③► In 200 yds take gate/stile (wm) on R. Cross field to stile (wm) and path on LH side of fence. Path forks twice (wm) – each time keep L uphill. Climb around wall-corner to ladder-stile. ④► Straight on to cross farm road and up to top of rocks (Foster's Leap). Pass wall-corner just beyond and keep straight ahead with wall on L. ⑤► At foot of steep descent go L over wall-stile (wm) then turn L (wm) to climb back up again! Follow wire fence to paved path (wm) into pub car park. Go R along road for a good half-mile. ⑥► Turn sharp R down to gate and cart-track. ⑦► In half-a-mile fork R off main track (FP Wycoller, Pendle Way) and follow wall to gate. Continue ahead, keeping fairly close to wall on L. Path eventually goes L through gate and drops to stream. ⑧► Ford stream, scramble up bank and at top turn R to gate/stile at wall-corner. Path gradually descends to stile close to stream. Cross next field and at its far end turn L and climb steep hillside to gate in wire fence near outcrops (View Point Rocks). ⑨► Turn R through gateway (wm) and stay parallel with wall on R to stile in crosswall (NOT the corner-stile on the R). ⑩► Turn L to crumbling wall and walk along its RH side. Keep straight on through two stiles and a gate, then follow a rushy ditch to a path between walls. ⑪► At its end take small gate on R and follow ditch towards farm. At end of ditch turn R and head for derelict farm, via two wall-stiles. Go through gate into farmyard and turn L along access road. ⑫► At crossroads of tracks (by gate) turn R. Head for conifers, keeping wall/fence/wall on your R. Path descends through edge of wood to lane down to Wycoller.

AN UNDULATING CIRCUIT OF THE LOVELY VALE OF WYCOLLER, ONE OF EAST LANCASHIRE'S BEST-LOVED BEAUTY SPOTS. MODERATELY STRENUOUS WITHOUT REACHING ANY GREAT ALTITUDE (MAX. 1145' AT HERDERS INN). MOSTLY ON WELL-WAYMARKED TRACKS AND PATHS. GENERALLY QUITE FIRM UNDERFOOT, WITH A FEW BOGGY BITS BETWEEN POINTS ⑦-⑧ AND ⑩-⑫. JUST OVER HALF-A-MILE ON A MOTOR-ROAD. 1 LADDER-STILE. SAFE IN MIST. MANY INTERESTING FEATURES.

4

! **WARNING**: THE FORD AT POINT ⑧ MAY BE A PROBLEM IF THE STREAM'S IN SPATE AFTER RAIN.

WYCOLLER, an ancient village rescued from seemingly inevitable dereliction, is one of Lancashire's prettiest and most romantic places. During the 17th and 18th centuries Wycoller became a thriving handloom weaving centre, but fell into decline when the invention of power looms took the textile industry to town mills. In the 1890s a proposal was made to create a reservoir by damming the beck near the aisled barn, but luckily the scheme was never implemented. In 1950 a society called 'Friends of Wycoller' was formed and began some restoration work on the then deserted and crumbling village. Despite this the chances of Wycoller's survival looked slim until, in 1973, renovation and maintenance were assured when Lancashire County Council bought the estate. **THINGS TO SEE**: PACKHORSE BRIDGE (illustrated) Possibly 13th C. CLAPPER BRIDGE Probably late 18th C. PIERSON'S HOUSE (illustrated) Named after family who lived here in 18th C. HALL Thought to be 'Ferndean Manor' of Charlotte Brontë's 'Jane Eyre'. Built 16th C. Extended 1744. Abandoned 1818. AISLED BARN Superb structure built 1630s. CLAM BRIDGE Short detour upstream from Aisled Barn. Single slab bridge, one of oldest in England. The village has a well-stocked GIFT SHOP / TEAROOM.

VACCARY WALLING Upright stone slabs erected to enclose a 'vaccary' (monastic cattle farm). The many examples seen on this walk were probably built in the 13th C.

FOSTER'S LEAP
TWO HUGE BOULDERS, SEPARATED BY A 6' GAP, NAMED AFTER ONE FOSTER CUNLIFFE WHO JUMPED SAFELY (SO IT IS SAID) FROM ONE BOULDER TO THE OTHER. HE MUST HAVE BEEN EITHER MAD OR DRUNK. DEFINITELY NOT RECOMMENDED.

The Herders Inn
This lonely inn stands on the Laneshaw Bridge to Haworth road. Once called the Oldham Arms, it has been a pub since 1860, but existed long before that.

COOMBE HILL CROSS
Reached by a sunken path (not a right-of-way) rising from a gate opposite Coombe Hill Cross Farm. Of uncertain origin, but obviously of great antiquity.

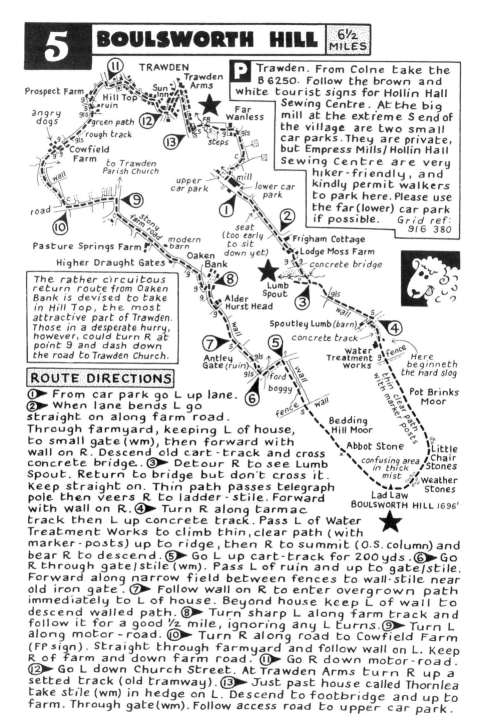

TRAWDEN

Trawden Arms

Sun Inn

Prospect Farm

Hill Top ruin

angry dogs

green path

rough track

Cowfield Farm

to Trawden Parish Church

wall

road

Pasture Springs Farm

Higher Draught Gates

modern barn

Oaken Bank

P Trawden. From Colne take the B6250. Follow the brown and white tourist signs for Hollin Hall Sewing Centre. At the big mill at the extreme S end of the village are two small car parks. They are private, but Empress Mills/Hollin Hall Sewing Centre are very hiker-friendly, and kindly permit walkers to park here. Please use the far (lower) car park if possible. *Grid ref: 916 380*

Far Wanless

FB

steps

upper car park

mill

lower car park

seat (too early to sit down yet)

Frigham Cottage

Lodge Moss Farm

concrete bridge

Lumb Spout

Alder Hurst Head

Spoutley Lumb (barn)

concrete track

Water Treatment Works

fence

Here beginneth the hard slog

Pot Brinks Moor

Bedding Hill Moor

Abbot Stone

confusing area in thick mist

Little Chair Stones

Weather Stones

Lad Law
BOULSWORTH HILL 1696'

Antley Gate (ruin)

ford boggy

fence

wall

The rather circuitous return route from Oaken Bank is devised to take in Hill Top, the most attractive part of Trawden. Those in a desperate hurry, however, could turn R at point 9 and dash down the road to Trawden Church.

ROUTE DIRECTIONS

①▶ From car park go L up lane. ②▶ When lane bends L go straight on along farm road. Through farmyard, keeping L of house, to small gate (wm), then forward with wall on R. Descend old cart-track and cross concrete bridge. ③▶ Detour R to see Lumb Spout. Return to bridge but don't cross it. Keep straight on. Thin path passes telegraph pole then veers R to ladder-stile. Forward with wall on R. ④▶ Turn R along tarmac track then L up concrete track. Pass L of Water Treatment Works to climb thin, clear path (with marker-posts) up to ridge, then R to summit (O.S. column) and bear R to descend. ⑤▶ Go L up cart-track for 200 yds. ⑥▶ Go R through gate/stile (wm). Pass L of ruin and up to gate/stile. Forward along narrow field between fences to wall-stile near old iron gate. ⑦▶ Follow wall on R to enter overgrown path immediately to L of house. Beyond house keep L of wall to descend walled path. ⑧▶ Turn sharp L along farm track and follow it for a good ½ mile, ignoring any L turns. ⑨▶ Turn L along motor-road. ⑩▶ Turn R along road to Cowfield Farm (FP sign). Straight through farmyard and follow wall on L. Keep R of farm and down farm road. ⑪▶ Go R down motor-road. ⑫▶ Go L down Church Street. At Trawden Arms turn R up a setted track (old tramway). ⑬▶ Just past house called Thornlea take stile (wm) in hedge on L. Descend to footbridge and up to farm. Through gate (wm). Follow access road to upper car park.

A STRENUOUS WALK FOR WHICH CLEAR WEATHER IS ESSENTIAL. THE NORTH WEST WATER AUTHORITY'S STEEP CONCESSIONARY FOOTPATH ALLOWS ACCESS TO THE TOP OF BOULSWORTH, THE SECOND HIGHEST POINT REACHED IN THIS BOOK. SOME BOGGY PATCHES WILL BE ENCOUNTERED ON THE MOOR. THE FINAL 2¾ MILES, FROM OAKEN BANK, IS MOSTLY ON ROADS AND FARM TRACKS. TWO LADDER-STILES (ONE WITH ADJACENT GATE). ¾ MILE ON QUIET MOTOR-ROADS. YOU ARE ASKED TO KEEP YOUR DOG ON A LEAD ON BOULSWORTH.

5

It's a waste of effort to climb Boulsworth in mist. If, on arriving at point 4, you can't see the hill, forget it and proceed along the broad track directly to point 5.

TRAWDEN

was a small, ancient settlement which expanded enormously during the reign of 'King Cotton'. The **HILL TOP** area, the oldest part of the village, is a delightfully haphazard jumble of 17th and 18th century buildings. The unprepossessing **PARISH CHURCH** was built 1845-6. Trawden's two pubs are as different as chalk and cheese. The **SUN INN**, a hostelry of immense character, dates back to the 18th C.; the late-Victorian **TRAWDEN ARMS** (until recently called the Rock Inn) was built in 1895 on the site of an old corn mill. The setted **TRAMWAY** running up from the Trawden Arms was opened 21-12-1905 to allow trams to bypass the main street which, beyond the Rock, was too narrow for them to negotiate. The last tram left Trawden 3-6-1928.

A Trawden tram of the 1920s.

LITTLE MOSS
unusual sign near point 9

BOULSWORTH'S summit ridge, with its clusters of bizarre gritstone outcrops, is a grand place to be on the right kind of day. The actual summit is called 'Lad Law', and an altar-shaped stone near the O.S. column is thought to have been used by Druids for sacrificial offerings.

LUMB SPOUT is a slender waterfall set in a lovely wooded hollow. In its heyday as a beauty spot there was a café here – the ruins can be seen just above the waterfall.

OAKEN BANK is a tiny hamlet, but there was a time when more than 100 people – many of them hand-loom weavers – lived here.

One of the Airstead herd of pedigree friesians based at the aptly named Cowfield Farm.

FAR WANLESS is an attractive early 17th C. house. The datestone (1753) above the door came from elsewhere and, in the owner's opinion, was probably placed here within the last 100 years. Prior to the Toleration Act of 1689 Far Wanless was secretly used as a Friends' Meeting House.

On completion of the walk award yourself a delicious afternoon tea, complete with scone, jam & cream, at BOBBINS CAFÉ

6 WUTHERING HEIGHTS 5¾ MILES

P Penistone Hill Country Park, to the W of Haworth. Park near its SW corner, just off the Stanbury – Oxenhope road (Moor Side Lane) where the O.S. map shows 'Tom Stell's Seat'. *Grid ref: 018 362*

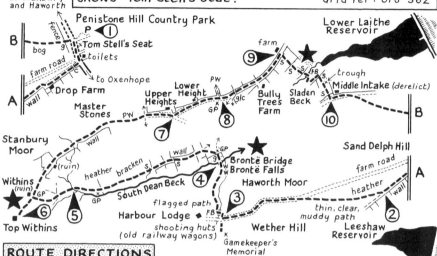

ROUTE DIRECTIONS

①► Walk L along road as far as a toilet block on the L. Opposite are two farm roads. Take the LH one by the wall (SP Brontë Falls, Top Withins). It ends at a house, but a clear path continues along the RH side of the wall. ②► When abreast of the reservoir on the L, fork R (SP Brontë Falls, Top Withins) onto a thin path in heather. At its end go L along farm road. ③► Just before reaching a stone bridge (with farm beyond) turn R (SP Brontë Falls, Top Withins) down to small footbridge. Cross it and turn R to follow a flagged path towards a shallow depression (ignore sign pointing L to Top Withins). Keep to LH side of ravine (care needed) and descend steeply to Brontë Bridge. ④► Cross it and climb stepped path (wm) to swing-gate. Fork L (SP Top Withins) up paved path. Follow clear path up valley. ⑤► Ford stream (stepping-stones) and climb paved path. At T-junction and guidepost turn L (SP Top Withins 200yds). ⑥► Return to guidepost and keep straight on (SP Stanbury Haworth, Pennine Way) on broad, level track. ⑦► Just past house on L (Upper Heights Farm) go L with wall (SP Pennine Way, Stanbury, Haworth). ⑧► At a guidepost the Pennine Way turns L, but our route keeps straight on, with wall on L. Cross cattle-grid and descend enclosed farm road. ⑨► At house on L turn R over stone stile and go straight down pastures to cross footbridge. Path goes R up bank then doubles back L up to ladder-stile. Climb field to ladder-stile at top LH corner. ⑩► Turn L along broad track. In 150yds, at a wm post, fork R onto a thin path which makes a beeline across the moor towards your parked car. Note: This last path has a boggy section at its far end. If you would rather avoid this, remain on the broad track to the Stanbury·Oxenhope road and turn R.

THIS WALK IS BEST DONE IN MIDWEEK, WHEN THE MOOR IS *RELATIVELY* QUIET – BUT YOU'LL SELDOM BE ALONE AT TOP WITHINS

A SPLENDID RAMBLE THROUGH QUINTESSENTIALLY SOUTH PENNINE GRITSTONE LANDSCAPES TO A LOCATION OF INTERNATIONAL FAME. CLEAR PATHS ALL THE WAY EXCEPT FOR THE SHORT SECTION BETWEEN POINTS ⑨ AND ⑩. SAFE – INDEED ATMOSPHERIC – IN MIST. IN ICE OR SNOW THE PATH ABOVE BRONTË FALLS IS POTENTIALLY DANGEROUS. 4 LADDER-STILES. MOTOR-ROAD WALKING NEGLIGIBLE.

6

NOTE FOR DOG-WALKERS. The last two ladder-stiles, just beyond the Sladen Beck footbridge, are tall and awkward to negotiate with a dog. To avoid this problem retrace steps from Top Withins to cross Brontë Bridge then turn L along the 'tourist path' to point ⑩.

✳ **PENISTONE HILL** is a designated Country Park, and its old quarries, which date from the 19th and early 20th centuries, now serve as car parks. Emily Brontë probably had this place in mind when she named the summit above Wuthering Heights 'Penistone Crags.'

A LITERARY PILGRIMAGE

When the Brontë family moved into Haworth Parsonage in 1820 there were 6 children under the age of 7 – MARIA (born 1814), ELIZABETH (1815), CHARLOTTE (1816), BRANWELL (1817), EMILY (1818) and ANNE (1820). Maria and Elizabeth both died of tuberculosis in 1825, aged 11 and 10 respectively, but the other 3 sisters achieved literary fame with classic novels such as 'JANE EYRE' (Charlotte, published 1847), 'WUTHERING HEIGHTS' (Emily 1847) and 'THE TENANT OF WILDFELL HALL' (Anne 1848). The sisters loved these bleak, harsh moors, and found inspiration here for

Emily Brontë

their writings. Thus it is entirely possible that the wild and austere setting of TOP WITHINS was in Emily's mind as she portrayed the lonely Earnshaw home in 'Wuthering Heights,' though, as the wall-plaque points out, this humble 18th C. dwelling would never have remotely resembled the fine Tudor yeoman farmer's house she described. In September 1848 Emily Brontë, whilst attending the funeral of her brother Branwell, caught a cold which developed into consumption, and she died on 19th December aged 30. Such is the popularity of her novel that year after year thousands of visitors

> **TOP WITHENS**
> THIS FARMHOUSE HAS BEEN ASSOCIATED WITH "WUTHERING HEIGHTS" THE EARNSHAW HOME IN EMILY BRONTË'S NOVEL
> THE BUILDINGS, EVEN WHEN COMPLETE, BORE NO RESEMBLANCE TO THE HOUSE SHE DESCRIBED,
> BUT THE SITUATION MAY HAVE BEEN IN HER MIND WHEN SHE WROTE OF THE MOORLAND SETTING OF THE HEIGHTS
> BRONTË SOCIETY 1964   THIS PLAQUE HAS BEEN PLACED HERE IN RESPONSE TO MANY INQUIRIES

trek to the grim ruins of Top Withins, which by now would have collapsed completely were it not for the preservation work of the Brontë Society. At its NE corner is a small, spidery room where you can shelter from the rain awhile before resuming your walk and getting drenched.

THE SISTERS' NOVELS ARE IMMENSELY POPULAR WITH THE JAPANESE, WHO VISIT HAWORTH IN LARGE NUMBERS TO SAVOUR THE 'BRONTË EXPERIENCE'. HENCE MANY SIGNS HAVE A JAPANESE TRANSLATION.

TOP WITHINS 1ml. 歩道

BRONTË BRIDGE is the prettiest place on the walk, and was a favourite haunt of Emily and Charlotte. The ancient structure was destroyed by flash floods on 19th May 1989 and rebuilt the following year. The nearby **FALLS** are on a tiny tributary beck, and are only impressive after very heavy rain.

● **SOUTH DEAN BECK** and **SLADEN BECK** are one and the same. ● **LEESHAW RESERVOIR** was built in 1879 and **LOWER LAITHE RESERVOIR** in 1926.

The stile at point ⑨

23

ROUTE DIRECTIONS

①▶ From car park entrance go L along lane. Cross main road to climb Dark Lane. At top of hill turn R along lane. **②▶** At crossroads turn L past Post Office. In 120 yds fork R along Jew Lane. Ignore minor lane forking R. When road curves L as 'Back Leeming' keep straight on down lane, which eventually becomes a slabbed path up to last house (Egypt). **③▶** Immediately past house go L over low stile to follow wall on L. Cross tarmac lane to stile (SP Brontë Way) and farm road. When it forks keep L through gate. At next gate turn L (SP Brontë Way) off farm road to stone stile (wm) into enclosed path. Keep straight on to reach wooden footbridge. **④▶** Keep straight on up into wooded stream-valley. Cross stone bridge and immediately turn R (wm) uphill. Cross stile and keep straight ahead up to ladder-stile and culvert. **⑤▶** Keep straight on alongside rushy, sunken path. When it ends turn L (wm) and in 40 yds at gatepost (wm) turn R uphill. Path soon bears L (BW sign) and climbs to a three-way signpost. Here leave the Brontë Way, which goes L. Go up to gate/stile into walled track. **⑥▶** Take metal gate on R and LH of two paths, which slants up hillside as a sunken way. At a crossroads of paths (with tips of wind-turbines just visible) go R on well-trodden path. Follow it through the quarries of Nab Hill and down to a stile. **⑦▶** Turn R down tarmac road. **⑧▶** Just beyond a mast take stile on L (FP sign). Follow wall to its far end and turn L up rough track. As it drops towards pub avoid the quagmire of its lower reaches by escaping into field on its R. **⑨▶** Cross road to concrete gateposts and descend enclosed track. Stay close to wall on R along top of Stones (a heathery escarpment). **⑩▶** At path junction go straight ahead (FP sign) along narrow path. At next junction turn L (FP sign) through wall-gap and follow wall on R. **⑪▶** Turn R along road. At junction turn L down a tarmac drive. Follow tarmac path through park, with playing fields on your L. At park exit turn L down road then R into Mill Lane

P Oxenhope. Car park at railway station.
Grid ref: 032 353

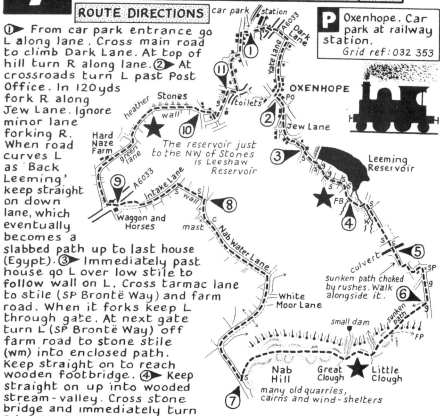

MODERATELY STRENUOUS. NO PARTICULARLY STEEP GRADIENTS, BUT LOTS OF MINOR UPS AND DOWNS. THE TERRAIN IS EXCEPTIONALLY VARIED, AND INCLUDES STREETS AND GINNELS, FIELD AND MOORLAND PATHS, TARMAC LANES AND OLD SUNKEN QUARRY TRACKS. THERE WILL BE NO SHORTAGE OF MUD IN WET WEATHER. EXTENSIVE VIEWS AND SOME INTERESTING CULVERT FEATURES, ESPECIALLY BY THE TRACK DOWN TO HARD NAZE FARM. ONLY 1 LADDER - STILE (AT POINT ⑤), BUT IT'S TALL AND MAY BE AWKWARD FOR DOG - WALKERS.

NOTE : FOR A REALLY MEMORABLE DAY OUT, START AT KEIGHLEY AND RIDE TO AND FROM THE WALK ON THE FAMOUS STEAM RAILWAY.

OXENHOPE

This large, hill - encircled village was once a centre for handloom - weaving and quarrying. From the walk here described a short, but worthwhile, detour is required to visit the **PARISH CHURCH OF ST. MARY THE VIRGIN**, which was built in 1849 but looks considerably older. The massive square tower, though only 44' high, has a tremendously imposing appearance.

THE STATIONS

KEIGHLEY

INGROW   1

tunnel

DAMEMS   2

3   OAKWORTH

tunnel

HAWORTH

4

Numbers denote miles from Keighley

5

OXENHOPE

Oxenhope's first vicar was the Revd. Joseph Brett Grant, who had previously been assistant curate to the Revd. Patrick Brontë (the Brontë sisters' dad) at Haworth. The church has a distinctly warm and friendly feel about it, and is obviously lovingly cared for by its parishioners.

Undoubtedy Oxenhope is best - known by association with the superbly restored and preserved **KEIGHLEY AND WORTH VALLEY RAILWAY**, of which it is the southern terminus. This 5-mile-long Midland Railway branch line, built in 1867 with the aid of funding by local mill-owners, closed down in 1962, but enthusiasts immediately sprang to the rescue by forming a Preservation Society. To ride the rails today is to experience the romance of a bygone era ; the pungent smell of smoke and steam and the nostalgia of traditional carriages, station gaslamps and blazing fires in cosy waiting rooms. Edith Nesbitt's novel 'The Railway Children' was filmed on location here in 1969 - 70, starring Jenny Agutter and Bernard Cribbins, and has become a celluloid classic. Steam trains run every weekend, and daily in summer and school holidays. For general enquiries ring 01535 645214.

THE RESERVOIRS

Hard Naze Farm

LEEMING RESERVOIR opened in 1879. On its far side stands Sykes Mill, which operated as a spinning mill from 1848 to the early 20th C. It is now converted into flats. On your L at point ⑥ is THORNTON MOOR RESERVOIR, completed in 1885. Ahead at point ⑦ is WARLEY MOOR RESERVOIR, better known locally as Fly Flat Reservoir.

shown as Hard Nese on the O.S. map

STONES IS A BEAUTIFUL, HEATHER-CLAD ESCARPMENT WHERE LOCAL DOGS LOVE TO EXERCISE THEIR OWNERS.

8 WIDDOP & GORPLE | 4 MILES | P Widdop Reservoir, on the Colne-

Hebden Bridge minor road. Parking area 125 yds E of dam.   Grid ref: 937 327

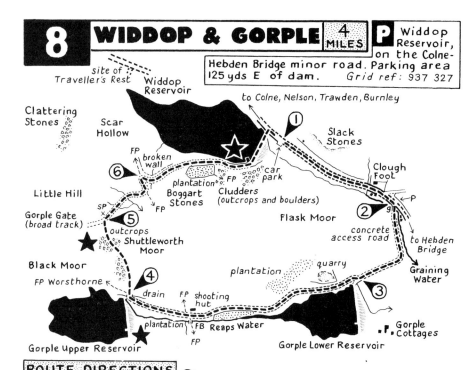

ROUTE DIRECTIONS ① From car park walk R (away from the reservoir) along road for just over ½ mile. ② At bottom of hill (small parking area on L) fork R (BW Lower Gorple) through gates and down double-strip concrete access road. ③ At dam take R fork (Permissive Footpath Upper Gorple). ④ Just before top of next dam turn R over concrete slab across a drain (SP Widdop). *Note: A short detour to the far end of the dam will provide a lovely view down valley to the Lower Reservoir and beyond.* Climb thin, clear path towards outcrops on skyline. ⑤ Beyond outcrops, at T-junction with broad track, turn R (SP Public Bridleway Widdop Road). ⑥ At a sharp RH bend a thin path goes straight ahead by a wall. This forms part of a permissive footpath circuit of the reservoir, but a dire boggy section makes it hardly worth the bovver. Instead, stay with the MAIN TRACK along the S side of the reservoir and across the dam.

! The narrow motor-road linking Colne and Hebden Bridge provides the motorist with a superbly scenic drive, but is DANGEROUS IN ICY CONDITIONS.

The combination of lake and moor provides an attractive habitat for a wide variety of birdlife. Keep a special lookout for three of our largest moorland birds – the buzzard, the raven and the curlew.

★

The illustration shows how steps have been built into a catchwater drain at Gorple Upper Reservoir to allow grouse chicks to cross the channel.

'grouse steps'

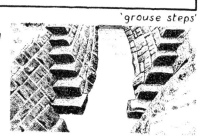

26

THE SHORTEST AND, IN DECENT CONDITIONS, THE EASIEST WALK IN THE BOOK, WITH GENTLE GRADIENTS AND A TOTAL ASCENT OF LESS THAN 500' BETWEEN POINTS ② AND ⑤ (THE SUMMIT OF THE WALK AT 1420'). SPLENDID GRITSTONE SCENERY. NO LADDER - STILES (IN FACT NO STILES AT ALL). JUST OVER ½ MILE ON A QUIET MOTOR - ROAD. CLEAR TRACKS AND PATHS THROUGHOUT MAKE THE WALK SAFE IN MIST, BUT THE LAST ¾ MILE, ALONG THE GORPLE GATE TRACK, CAN BE EXECRABLY MUDDY AFTER PROLONGED RAIN, AND THE WALK SHOULD NOT BE UNDERESTIMATED IN BAD WEATHER. THIS IS WILD, EXPOSED MOORLAND TERRAIN, AND IS BEST AVOIDED IN SEVERE WINTRY CONDITIONS.

the valve house

THE RESERVOIRS

If a poll were to be held to establish which of the region's many reservoirs is the most beautiful, it is probable that the vote would go to **WIDDOP**. In its wild and colourful setting of steep, boulder-strewn and bracken-clad slopes topped by dark, bristling crags it is reminiscent of a large Lakeland tarn. Widdop (the name means 'wide valley') Reservoir was built to supply Halifax, and materials were transported to the site up a 5½ mile-long horse-drawn tramway from Shackleton. A shanty-town, known locally as 'Navvyopolis', was established at Widdop to cater for the navvies and their families. The temporary settlement had about two dozen huts, a general store, a bakehouse and a reading room, and at peak activity some 200 men were working on the project. The reservoir was completed in 1878, covers 93 acres and holds 633 million gallons of water. The engineer Edward Bateman had attended the opening ceremony of the Suez Canal in 1869, and there is a certain Egyptian character in his design of the valve house at the south end of the dam.

The two **GORPLE RESERVOIRS** were constructed in the 1930s. They are much smaller than Widdop and don't have the same visual appeal, being more stark in setting and more obviously artificial.

★

GORPLE GATE is an old packhorse way over the moors to Worsthorne in Lancashire, and would once have been a major trade route.

THE TRAVELLER'S REST INN (see map) WAS, IN THE EARLY 19TH C, THE HEADQUARTERS OF A DESPERATE GANG OF ROBBERS WHO MADE A HABIT OF RAIDING HOUSES ACROSS THE BORDER IN LANCASHIRE. THE INN WAS CLOSED DOWN IN 1891 WHEN IT WAS FOUND TO BE OPERATING AN ILLEGAL GAMBLING SCHOOL.

CLUDDERS means 'mass of rocks', and is the name given to the crags and weirdly-shaped outcrops above Widdop's southern shore. There are some quite challenging rock climbs here.

CLOUGH FOOT is a somewhat sombre-looking house. John Wesley, the founder of Methodism, is said to have preached here. In the mid-19thC. this was the home of old Sally Walton, well-known locally as a reputed witch.

John Wesley
1703 - 1791

9 WADSWORTH MOOR

P Clough Foot. Small car park by the Colne – Hebden Bridge minor road ½ mile NW of Pack Horse Inn.

Grid ref: 947 323

ROUTE DIRECTIONS

①► Walk along road towards distant white building (Pack Horse Inn). ②► 100 yds beyond Well Hole Cottage go R through gate (PW sign) into walled path. Go L with wall. Ignore flagged path descending R. When wall ends a clear path continues, running below large outcrops to meet a road at a hairpin bend. ③► Go down road. At first bend go L (FP sign) along grassy drive. Take gate on R (Path to Streamside), cross footbridge and climb stepped path. ④► At path junction go R along broad green path. From stile a thin path runs through bracken and into woodland. 25 yds past a wall-corner path crosses to LH side of wall. ⑤► Pass a house and keep straight on along broad woodland track. ⑥► Turn sharp L up path to pass through small gateway in short length of wall. Climb steeply. Just before reaching a wooden stile double back L to small gate in wall (easily missed). Go straight up field to pass through gate near tall weathervane. Cross corner stile into hamlet. ⑦► Three tracks leave hamlet. Take middle one, immediately to R of detached house. ⑧► Turn R (SP Walshaw Dean Permissive Path) up to gate. Climb broad track by wall on L. ⑨► At top of enclosed track go straight up thin path. Rejoin broad track and follow it straight ahead over moor. At a shooting hut it swings L to head for dam of middle reservoir. ⑩► Cross dam and go L along tarmac reservoir road. In places a fenced walkers' path runs alongside it. ⑪► Just before reaching motor-road take gate on L and follow wall L to car park.

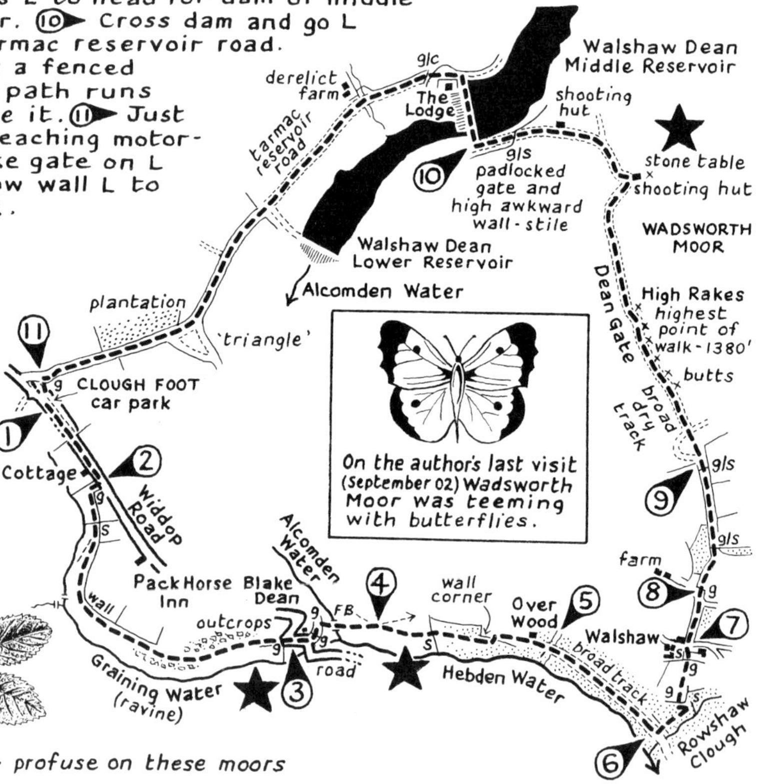

[Map with the following labels:]

g/c
derelict farm
The Lodge
tarmac reservoir road
Walshaw Dean Middle Reservoir
shooting hut
⑩
g/s padlocked gate and high awkward wall-stile
★ stone table × shooting hut
WADSWORTH MOOR
Walshaw Dean Lower Reservoir
plantation
Alcomden Water
High Rakes highest point of walk - 1380'
butts
Dean Gate
broad dry track
⑪
'triangle'
g CLOUGH FOOT car park
①
Well Hole Cottage
②
Widdop Road
wall
Pack Horse Inn
Blake Dean
outcrops
Graining Water (ravine)
③ ★
Alcomden Water
road
④ FB
wall corner
Over Wood
⑤
Walshaw
broad track
Hebden Water
g/s
g/s
⑨
farm
⑧ g
⑦ s/g
g s
⑥ Rowshaw Clough

On the author's last visit (September 02) Wadsworth Moor was teeming with butterflies.

Bilberry – profuse on these moors

28

DEFINITELY ONE OF THE BEST WALKS IN THE BOOK. RAVINE, WOODLAND, RIVERSIDE AND MOORLAND SCENERY OF STUNNING BEAUTY, WITH THE ADDED BONUS OF AN ABSENCE OF PYLONS. THE WALK IS MODERATELY STRENUOUS, WITH SEVERAL CLIMBS — SOME OF THEM QUITE STEEP. NO LADDER-STILES, BUT A VERY HIGH WALL-STILE NEAR POINT 10 COULD PRESENT A DOG DIFFICULTY. ¼ MILE ON A QUIET MOTOR-ROAD. SAFE IN MIST.

9

! The moorland track between Walshaw and the reservoirs (points 7-10) is a PERMISSIVE PATH on Savile Estate land, and may be closed on certain days between 12 Aug and 10 Dec for grouse shooting. On such occasions red flags are flown at the start of the path. CALDERDALE COUNTRYSIDE SERVICE (01422 359454) or HEBDEN BRIDGE T.I.C. (01422 843831) may be able to provide advance details of closure dates. If you DO get caught out, you can avoid getting shot by taking the LH track at Walshaw (point 7), which leads directly to the 'triangle' (see map).

★BLAKE DEAN, with its steep

and colourful bracken-clad and boulder-strewn slopes, is a renowned BEAUTY SPOT. Here the road climbs tortuously out of the valley in a series of acute hairpin bends, at one of which (point 3) stands a tree-shaded and somewhat forlorn-looking building. It now announces itself as a SCOUT HOSTEL, but it was built in 1802 as a BAPTIST CHAPEL, and its long-neglected BURIAL GROUND still survives. Below the chapel we cross a FOOTBRIDGE at a pretty WATERSMEET, and hereabouts the course of an old (1901) RAILWAY is clearly visible. Steam locomotives hauled materials up to the reservoir site in WALSHAW DEAN, crossing the valley on a huge trestle bridge some 700' long and 105' high. Remains of its stone foundations can be seen in the stream bed. The bridge and track were dismantled in 1912.

Over Wood

This lonely house dates back to the 17th C., but has recently been substantially rebuilt after suffering severe fire damage.

WALSHAW, a farming hamlet. The house with the impressive frontage seen on the approach from point 6 was built in the 1860s as a shooting lodge for Lord Savile.

THE RESERVOIRS

Construction of the Walshaw Dean reservoirs began in 1900, and the official opening took place in 1907, but leakage problems meant that the project was not completed until 1915. At the peak of activity the work-force numbered over 500 men. Flocks of Canada geese can sometimes be seen here.

This stone table can be found behind the first shooting hut on the descent to the reservoirs. On a sunny day, with the heather in bloom, it's a superb picnic place.

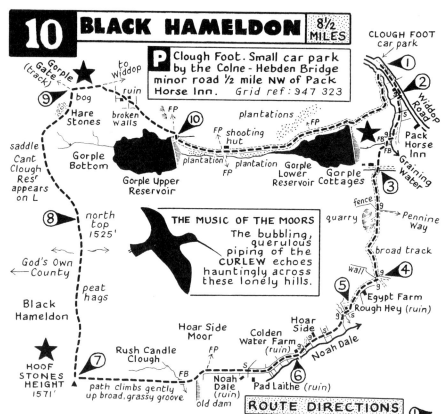

P Clough Foot. Small car park by the Colne - Hebden Bridge minor road ½ mile NW of Pack Horse Inn. *Grid ref: 947 323*

CLOUGH FOOT car park

THE MUSIC OF THE MOORS

The bubbling, querulous piping of the CURLEW echoes hauntingly across these lonely hills.

ROUTE DIRECTIONS

① Walk along road towards distant white building (Pack Horse Inn). ② 100 yds beyond Well Hole Cottage turn R through gate (PW sign) into walled path. Go L with wall, and when path forks go R downhill. Cross two footbridges and follow path climbing R by old wall. ③ Cross bridge over drain and ascend broad track. At a gate ignore PW sign pointing L. Stay on broad track over moor. ④ Through gate and turn sharp R through gate/stile. Follow farm road past Egypt Farm. ⑤ Approaching a ruin locate a wall-stile to its L. Cross small footbridge to gate and turn L. Sketchy path (old causeway) soon swings R and heads towards farm. Pass below farm, on a level course, to a small gate, then join broad track to descend to a ruined farmhouse (Colden Water Farm). ⑥ Follow track between old walls to its end at a stile. Keep straight on alongside wall on L. Beyond this wall the route to the summit (O.S. column) is clearly waymarked. ⑦ At O.S. column turn R. The obvious line of an old ditch stretches ahead along the ridge, and a very sketchy path runs along its RH side. When it gets a bit vague, just keep straight on (due N). ⑧ As path begins to descend from north top it swings L down a stony depression. Path gets clearer as it drops to a saddle, then rises to pass R of prominent outcrops. ⑨ Turn R along broad bridleway (Gorple Gate). In 300 yds fork R (short marker-post) down clear path which passes through some ruins and descends to reservoir dam. ⑩ Cross concrete bridge over drain and go L down reservoir road – 1¾ miles to car park.

IN THE RIGHT CONDITIONS THIS IS ONE OF THE FINEST 'WILDERNESS WALKS' IN THE SOUTH PENNINES, BUT IT SHOULD CERTAINLY NOT BE UNDERESTIMATED. THERE ARE NO REALLY STEEP GRADIENTS, BUT THE ROUGH, TUSSOCKY GRASS ON THE ASCENT FROM NOAH DALE IS POTENTIALLY ANKLE-TWISTING, AND THE PEATY GROUND ALONG THE RIDGE CAN BE SERIOUSLY SOGGY. DON'T ATTEMPT THE WALK IN MIST, AND BEAR IN MIND ALSO THAT IN FOUL WEATHER THERE IS NO VESTIGE OF SHELTER BETWEEN COLDEN WATER FARM AND HARE STONES. NO LADDER-STILES. MOTOR-ROAD WALKING NEGLIGIBLE.

Pack Horse Inn

This ancient hostelry stands by the Widdop road – not directly on our route, but thirst may induce a brief detour.

The lonely and sombre-looking **GORPLE COTTAGES** will always be associated with a 1960's tragedy, when the resident reservoir keeper was caught in a severe blizzard and perished on the moors he knew so well.

The reservoir above the cottages is the lower of a pair built to serve Halifax and completed in 1934. We shall pass its twin later on the walk. The two reservoirs each have a surface area of just over 50 acres.

NOAH DALE

is a study in dereliction – a melancholy place of crumbling stone walls and the forlorn ruins of farmsteads which were probably established in the early 1800s. Farming these inhospitable moors would never have been a very lucrative occupation, and the meagre profits would in most cases have been augmented by a secondary income from handloom-weaving.

BLACK HAMELDON

(the name means black scarred hill) is a lofty and peaty ridge of rough moorland forming part of the Pennine watershed. Its highest point, at its southern end, rejoices in the name 'Hoof Stones Height', and is marked by an O.S. column. At 1571' it is, in terms of altitude, one of this book's 'Big Four' – one of four summits exceeding 1500'. The others are Pendle Hill (1831'), Boulsworth Hill (1696') and Blackstone Edge (1548'). The broadness of the ridge partially obscures the Calder valley, but there are fine views northwards to the Yorkshire Dales and to the west across England's finest county, with dear old Pendle particularly prominent. Surprisingly close at hand are the ghostly turbines of Coal Clough windfarm.

Brandy Keighley at Hoof Stones Height

GORPLE GATE was an important packhorse route ('gate' is an old name for a track) from Worsthorne in Lancashire to Heptonstall. Lime and cloth came this way.

During summer months look out for the **COMMON LIZARD** (Lacerta vivipara), particularly on south-facing slopes. This grey or brown reptile is about 5" long (½ of which is tail) and feeds chiefly on insects, spiders and caterpillars.

11 HURSTWOOD & WORSTHORNE

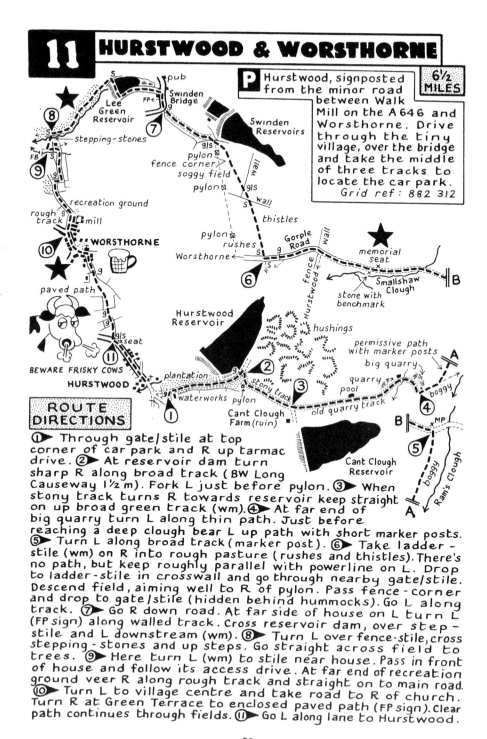

P Hurstwood, signposted from the minor road between Walk Mill on the A646 and Worsthorne. Drive through the tiny village, over the bridge and take the middle of three tracks to locate the car park. *Grid ref: 882 312*

6½ MILES

ROUTE DIRECTIONS

① Through gate/stile at top corner of car park and R up tarmac drive. ② At reservoir dam turn sharp R along broad track (BW Long Causeway 1½ m). Fork L just before pylon. ③ When stony track turns R towards reservoir keep straight on up broad green track (wm). ④ At far end of big quarry turn L along thin path. Just before reaching a deep clough bear L up path with short marker posts. ⑤ Turn L along broad track (marker post). ⑥ Take ladder-stile (wm) on R into rough pasture (rushes and thistles). There's no path, but keep roughly parallel with powerline on L. Drop to ladder-stile in crosswall and go through nearby gate/stile. Descend field, aiming well to R of pylon. Pass fence-corner and drop to gate/stile (hidden behind hummocks). Go L along track. ⑦ Go R down road. At far side of house on L turn L (FP sign) along walled track. Cross reservoir dam, over step-stile and L downstream (wm). ⑧ Turn L over fence-stile, cross stepping-stones and up steps. Go straight across field to trees. ⑨ Here turn L (wm) to stile near house. Pass in front of house and follow its access drive. At far end of recreation ground veer R along rough track and straight on to main road. ⑩ Turn L to village centre and take road to R of church. Turn R at Green Terrace to enclosed paved path (FP sign). Clear path continues through fields. ⑪ Go L along lane to Hurstwood.

32

11

THIS EASY RAMBLE OFFERS A WIDE DIVERSITY OF LANDSCAPES AND AN OPPORTUNITY TO EXPLORE TWO HISTORIC VILLAGES NESTLING AT THE FOOT OF THE BLEAK MOORS EAST OF BURNLEY. CONSIDERING THAT A HEIGHT OF 1300' IS ATTAINED (AT POINT ⑤) THE GRADIENTS ARE SURPRISINGLY GENTLE, AND THE WALK IS MOSTLY ON CLEAR TRACKS AND PATHS, WITH JUST ONE PATHLESS STRETCH 'TWIXT GORPLE ROAD AND SWINDEN RESERVOIR. THE MOORLAND PATH BETWEEN POINTS ④ AND ⑤ HAS A FEW BOGGY PATCHES, AND IN WET WEATHER THE SWINDEN SECTION IS ALL MUD AND COW MUCK. THE STEPPING-STONES AT POINT ⑧ MAY BE UNUSABLE AFTER HEAVY RAIN; IF SO RETURN TO POINT ⑦ AND FOLLOW THE ROAD (1 MILE) INTO WORSTHORNE. 2 LADDER-STILES. ⅓ MILE ON QUIET MOTOR-ROADS.

TWO SHORT CUTS ARE AVAILABLE. IF YOU'RE PUSHED FOR TIME OR ALLERGIC TO COW MUCK, YOU MAY OMIT THE SWINDEN SECTION BY KEEPING STRAIGHT ON AT POINT ⑥ TO FOLLOW THE GORPLE ROAD INTO WORSTHORNE, REDUCING THE WALK TO 4¾ MILES. IF YOU'RE JIGGERED OR TOTALLY BRASSED-OFF TURN L 600 YDS PAST THE MEMORIAL SEAT DOWN A SIGNPOSTED PATH TO HURSTWOOD.

The construction of **HURSTWOOD RESERVOIR** began in 1908 but was not completed until 1925, progress having been interrupted by the Great War. Coniferous plantations enhance its visual appeal. The older **CANT CLOUGH RESERVOIR** (1876) has a much more stark and harsh appearance.

★

The weird and tortured landscape above these reservoirs is the result of '**HUSHING**', an old (pre-19th C) method of extracting buried limestone. A complex of small canals was dug to drain surface water into dammed ponds. The water was then released in a torrent to gouge away the topsoil of clay and sand.

WORSTHORNE is a village of ancient origin. You'll find its most famous feature, the 'RED MAN', just past the RH end of the row of white shops in the village centre. The figure is a pun on the name of Frank Redman, who built these houses in the 1860s. Opposite the shops is an ornate gaslamp. It stands on a stone pedestal, and is locally known as the 'GORMLESS.' The somewhat austere appearance of the CHURCH (1835) rather belies its lovely and well-cared-for interior. The two pubs – the BAY HORSE and the CROOKED BILLET – have both been rebuilt – in 1899 and 1913 respectively – on the sites of much older inns. These few brief notes are all that space in this book will allow, but an excellent booklet, 'Worsthorne Village Trail', is obtainable in the village.

chapel gate

HURSTWOOD is an absolute gem. HURSTWOOD HALL, in the centre of the hamlet, dates from 1579. Though much altered, it remains a fine example of Tudor architecture. To its R, and of similar vintage, is the splendid SPENSER'S HOUSE, home between 1576 and 1578 of the poet Edmund Spenser (1552-99). Just inside the chapel gates (pictured L) is the grave of Richard Collinge, who was organist here for an incredible 70 years. The stream is the infant River Brun, from which Burnley takes its name.

THE LIFE GATE

12 OGDEN WATER & OVENDEN MOOR 6¾ MILES

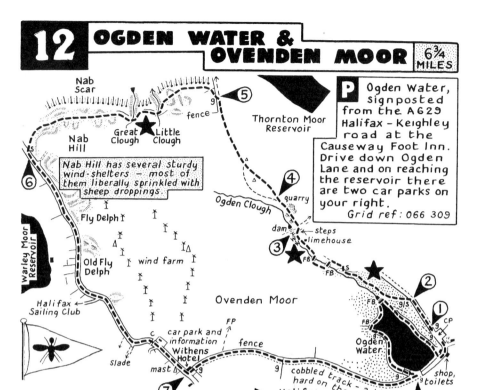

Nab Scar

Nab Hill

Great Clough Little Clough

fence

⑤

Thornton Moor Reservoir

P Ogden Water, signposted from the A629 Halifax – Keighley road at the Causeway Foot Inn. Drive down Ogden Lane and on reaching the reservoir there are two car parks on your right.
Grid ref: 066 309

Nab Hill has several sturdy wind-shelters – most of them liberally sprinkled with sheep droppings.

Fly Delph

④

Ogden Clough quarry

dam steps limehouse

③ ★ FB

Warley Moor Reservoir

Old Fly Delph wind farm

Ovenden Moor

② ① CP

FB

Halifax Sailing Club

car park and information FP fence

Withens Hotel

Slade mast

⑦

cobbled track – a bit hard on the feet

shop, toilets

⑧

Halifax Golf Club

Ogden Water

ROUTE DIRECTIONS

①▶ Go to far end of lower car park and take swing-gate by large metal gate to broad track above trees. ②▶ At a stone-walling display area go L through gate/stile to descending woodland path. Don't go L across footbridge. Keep to R of water. Path comes alongside stream as it enters narrow confines of Ogden Clough. Follow stream up, crossing and re-crossing it via two footbridges, to reach an old dam. ③▶ Don't cross dam. Turn R up stone steps and at top turn L to follow broad path high above clough. ④▶ Just past a small quarry on your R the path forks. Keep R along broad, rutted track. Eventually a fence materialises on your L. ⑤▶ Cross this fence through a swing-gate and head away along a clear path (not shown on O.S. map). Path keeps close to escarpment on R, skirts the heads of two cloughs and develops into a sunken quarry track before dropping to stile onto tarmac lane. ⑥▶ Turn L and follow this lane (it's not continuously tarmacked) for almost 1½ miles. ⑦▶ At Withens Hotel turn L across car park to gate. Follow the broad track (BW Ogden Water) down to reservoir dam. For short finish keep straight on across dam. ⑧▶ For full walk turn L to follow lakeside path. Two footbridges are crossed, and just beyond the second a path marked 'Woodland Trail' branches L. This leads directly back to the car park. If you wish to call at the Visitor Centre remain on the lakeside path, which passes en route a very pleasant little picnic area overlooking the lake.

PLEASE KEEP FIDO ON A LEAD ON THE LAKESIDE PATH

A REMARKABLE FEATURE OF THIS WALK IS ITS SUDDEN TRANSFIGURATION AT POINT ③. AFTER SAVOURING THE DELIGHTFUL WOODLANDS OF OGDEN WATER AND THE COLOURFUL CONFINES OF OGDEN CLOUGH, THE WALKER HERE ENCOUNTERS A FLIGHT OF STONE STEPS WHICH CONVEY HIM, WITHIN A COUPLE OF MINUTES, FROM SHELTERED VALLEY TO EXPOSED, WINDSWEPT MOORLAND. THIS FLIGHT OF STEPS IS THE ONLY STEEP SECTION OF AN OTHERWISE EASY WALK. GOOD, CLEAR PATHS MAKE NAVIGATION SIMPLE, ALTHOUGH THICK MIST COULD CAUSE SOME CONFUSION AMONG THE OLD QUARRIES ON NAB HILL. THE MOORLAND STRETCH (POINTS ③ - ⑥) CAN BE MUDDY, BUT THERE ARE NO REAL BOGGY BITS. NO LADDER-STILES OR MOTOR-ROADS (THE ROAD BETWEEN POINTS ⑥ AND ⑦, ALTHOUGH IT *DOES* CARRY SOME TRAFFIC, CANNOT REALLY BE CLASSED AS A MOTOR-ROAD).

OGDEN WATER

is a local beauty spot, a dog-walker's delight, a birdwatcher's paradise and one of the region's most attractive reservoirs. Ogden's woodland trails and picnic areas make it well-worth a visit in its own right, even should you lack the time, energy or inclination to do an extended walk. The reservoir was built between 1854 and 1858, covers an area of 34½ acres and holds just over 220 million gallons. The woodlands were planted in 1905, and the predominant tree is Scots pine, with larch, beech, silver birch and sycamore also common.

footbridge, Ogden Clough

THORNTON MOOR RESERVOIR was completed in 1885. It covers 45 acres and holds 175 million gallons.

WARLEY MOOR RESERVOIR is 13 years older and has a surface area of 68 acres.

The twenty-three turbines of the **WIND FARM** provide eerily silent and rather ghostly company for much of the walk. Built in 1993, the towers are 105' high and each blade is 56' long. Detailed information is on display at the car park above the Withens Hotel.

Blade

Hub

←Nacelle

Yaw System *(whatever that is)*

Tower

Control Room

Transformer

To local Grid System

Underground Cable

Further upstream is a small ruined building where lime was once stored. The lime was put into the stream to reduce the acidity of the water.

WITHENS HOTEL

was established in 1862 to cater for local quarrymen, and, at 1321', claims to be the highest pub in W. Yorkshire. It is reputed to have been haunted since Victorian times by the ghost of a man who, after losing his way on the moor, staggered into the bar and dropped dead.

13 HARDCASTLE CRAGS 5¼ MILES

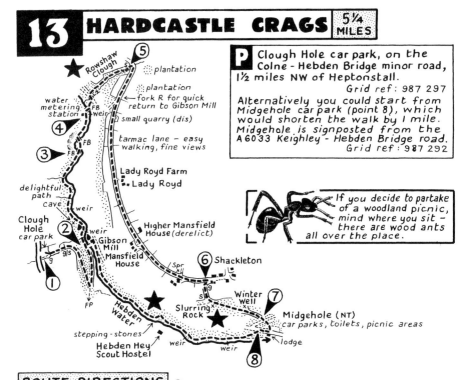

P Clough Hole car park, on the Colne - Hebden Bridge minor road, 1½ miles NW of Heptonstall.
Grid ref: 987 297
Alternatively you could start from Midgehole car park (point 8), which would shorten the walk by 1 mile. Midgehole is signposted from the A 6033 Keighley - Hebden Bridge road.
Grid ref: 987 292

If you decide to partake of a woodland picnic, mind where you sit — there are wood ants all over the place.

ROUTE DIRECTIONS ① From car park info. board go down stepped path and descend wide track. It executes a hairpin bend and drops to the bridge at Gibson Mill. ② DON'T cross bridge. Keep straight on along broad path to pass between two millponds. Continue upstream. ③ Cross river at footbridge then re-cross it at another (NOTE: These bridges can be very slippery in wet weather). ④ Cross a third footbridge and follow broad path away from river. Cross stone bridge over tributary stream and immediately turn R through gap in wall. Climb — steeply at first - clear path up LH side of stream. At top of clough cross two small bridges to reach wall-stile. ⑤ Turn R along lane and follow it for about 1¼ miles. ⑥ Just before first cottage (Hawthorn Cottage) at Shackleton turn sharp R through metal gate and follow wall on L to path between walls. From stile at bottom keep L, passing a huge boulder (Slurring Rock) on your R. Descend paved path which eventually becomes enclosed. ⑦ Keep R at car park, pass to R of info. board and cross road to descend path to lower car park. Turn R up tarmac road. ⑧ In about 40yds fork L down broad path to reach river bank. Follow riverside path upstream to Gibson Mill. Cross bridge and return up 'hairpin' track to car park.

PS THIS ROUTE IS IDEAL FOR DOGGIE-WALKIES, THERE BEING NO LADDER-STILES, MOTOR-ROADS, FARMYARDS OR FARM LIVESTOCK.

PPS BEAR IN MIND THAT HARDCASTLE CRAGS IS A TOURIST 'HONEYPOT', AND IS NORMALLY VERY BUSY AT WEEKENDS AND BANK HOLIDAYS.

THIS IS THE PRETTIEST WALK IN THE BOOK, WITH GLORIOUS WOODLAND AND RIVER SCENERY. GENERALLY VERY EASY WALKING, BUT THERE'S A SHORT, STEEP CLIMB INTO ROWSHAW CLOUGH AND YOU MAY FIND THE FINAL PULL UP TO THE CAR PARK A TAD TIRESOME (THE LATTER OF COURSE CAN BE AVOIDED BY STARTING AT MIDGEHOLE). CLEAR PATHS THROUGHOUT MEAN THERE ARE NO ROUTE-FINDING PROBLEMS, BUT WHEN THE WALK WAS RESEARCHED (Dec 01) THE PATH IN ROWSHAW CLOUGH SEEMED IN DANGER OF BECOMING OVERGROWN BY RHODODENDRONS.

! THE MINOR ROAD BETWEEN COLNE AND CLOUGH HOLE IS DANGEROUS IN ICY CONDITIONS

HARDCASTLE CRAGS

is the name by which the valley of Hebden Water, or Hebden Dale, is universally known, which seems rather odd when in fact the so-called 'crags' are merely a few unremarkable gritstone outcrops. On a knoll upstream of Gibson Mill, and largely obscured by vegetation, they can very easily be passed unnoticed. The valley as a whole, however, is so spectacularly beautiful that it surely couldn't fail to impress even the most blasé of visitors. This heavily-wooded gorge, through which Hebden Water gurgles and tumbles along its rocky bed, has long been loved by Yorkshire and Lancashire folk. In the days when King Cotton ruled the region Hardcastle Crags was a popular venue for weary millworkers out from their grimy towns in search of some greenery and fresh air. 'The Switzerland of the North' it was called in those days, and excursion trains brought hundreds of visitors to Hebden Bridge station every weekend. Hardcastle Crags has been in the care of the National Trust since 1950, and large crowds still flock here to enjoy the idyllic paths winding through woodlands which are among the oldest in the Pennines

Fast-flowing Hebden Water makes an ideal habitat for the DIPPER. This plump little bird, with its conspicuous white 'bib', can often be seen bobbing and bowing on mid-stream boulders. The dipper is unique among British birds in that it has perfected the trick of walking underwater.

GIBSON MILL

This imposing cotton mill, with its row of workers' cottages, was built by Abraham Gibson in 1800. Originally a watermill, and converted to steam in 1852, Gibson Mill was infamous for its harsh working conditions. In the 1830s a male worker earned 17s for a 72 hour week, women received 6s 6d for the same hours, and children as young as 10 toiled from 6 am to 7·30 pm for 2s 6d a week. Production ceased in the 1890s, since when the mill has enjoyed several re-incarnations as a dance hall, restaurant and roller-skating rink.

* ROWSHAW CLOUGH, also known as Cherry Hole Clough, has a delightful waterfall and was at one time laid out as an ornamental water-garden. In its upper reaches the path is sometimes muddy and slippery.

SLURRING ROCK

'SLURRING' IS A LOCAL WORD FOR 'SLIDING'. SLURRING ROCK IS A HUGE BOULDER WITH GROOVES WORN SMOOTH BY THE CLOG-IRONS OF GENERATIONS OF YOUNGSTERS SLIDING, OR SLURRING, DOWN ITS ANGLED SURFACE. THE OLD PANNIER-TRACK DESCENDING FROM HERE TO MIDGEHOLE IS KNOWN AS WILLOW GATE.

Hawthorn Cottage Shackleton

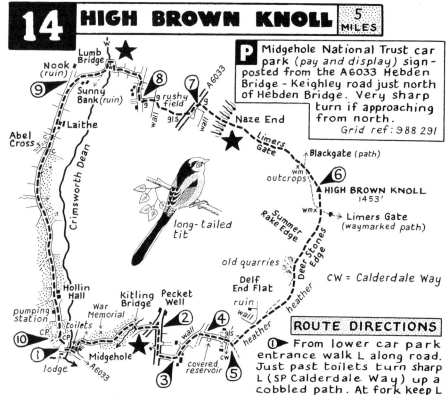

P Midgehole National Trust car park (*pay and display*) sign-posted from the A6033 Hebden Bridge - Keighley road just north of Hebden Bridge. Very sharp turn if approaching from north.
Grid ref: 988 291

long-tailed tit

CW = Calderdale Way

ROUTE DIRECTIONS

① From lower car park entrance walk L along road. Just past toilets turn sharp L (SP Calderdale Way) up a cobbled path. At fork keep L (BW Pecket Well). Path soon swings R to climb through woodland, levels out to cross a bridge, then climbs again. **②** Cross road to short path (wm) up to another road and turn R. Turn L up Shawcroft Hill (cw). **③** At houses go L into walled green path (wm). At fork keep R (straight on) uphill, with wall on your L. **④** Cross rough track and go up walled farm road (SP Old Town Slack Farm) On reaching open moor go ½ R up broad track (NOT cw path along wall-side). **⑤** In 50yds take second of two parallel sunken paths slanting L up hillside. Just beyond a wall-corner the path forks. Keep R. From brow of moor follow a clear, level, well-trodden path. Ignore any paths branching L. In clear weather the distant O.S. column on High Brown Knoll will now be visible. **⑥** At O.S. column keep straight on along clear path heading NW. Ignore a R fork. Path eventually drops steeply to roadside gate. **⑦** Go L along road to gate/stile on R (BW Haworth Old Road). Path runs slightly L down rushy field, swinging R at bottom to gate and descending wallside path. **⑧** Turn R along tarmac lane. In 200yds fork L (BW sign) down wallside path. Cross bridge. Downstream path soon turns R and becomes walled as it climbs steeply. Just above some ruins on the L the path bears L to rise to a junction. **⑨** Turn L along farm road and follow it for 1¼ downhill miles (just past a cattle-grid note the two Abel Crosses in a field on the R). **⑩** Just past the upper car park turn L down stepped path to lower car park.

ARRIVE EARLY ON SUMMER WEEKENDS AND BANK HOLIDAYS. MIDGEHOLE IS AN EXTREMELY POPULAR CAR PARK.

STRADDLING THE A6033, THIS SPLENDID RAMBLE OFFERS SUCH CONTRASTING TERRAIN THAT THE AUTHOR THINKS OF IT AS THE 'CHALK AND CHEESE WALK'. EAST OF THE ROAD IT IS ALL WILD, WINDSWEPT MOORLAND. WEST OF THE ROAD IS THE DEEP, WOODED AND DELECTABLE VALLEY OF CRIMSWORTH DEAN BOASTING — AT LUMB BRIDGE — ONE OF THE REGION'S MOST EXQUISITE BEAUTY SPOTS. THE WALK IS FAIRLY STRENUOUS, WITH TWO STEEPISH CLIMBS OUT OF THE VALLEY, AND SEEMS LONGER THAN 5 MILES. NO LADDER-STILES. MOTOR-ROAD WALKING NEGLIGIBLE. CLEAR PATHS THROUGHOUT, BUT HIGH BROWN KNOLL IS BEST AVOIDED IN BAD WEATHER.

WADSWORTH WAR MEMORIAL
On the way up to Kitling Bridge you will catch glimpses of a tall obelisk perched among the trees high on your left. This remarkable edifice was erected in memory of those from the parish who lost their lives in the service of their country.

PECKET WELL
is an old mill village which may be visited by making a short detour left at point ②. Here you will find a most welcoming pub - the Robin Hood Inn - as well as Britain's only remaining mill still producing fustian, a coarse cotton fabric used in corduroy.

The summit of High Brown Knoll, here in use as a fell race checkpoint (16-2-02)

HIGH BROWN KNOLL
is the second highest point (after Nab Hill) of the rolling moors between the A6033 and the A629. The summit itself is featureless save for an O.S. column, but as a viewpoint presents a vast panorama ranging from Penyghent in the north to Blackstone Edge in the south, and including Pendle Hill and Boulsworth (NW), Black Hameldon, Widdop and Gorple Reservoirs (W), Stoodley Pike (SW) and Warley Moor Reservoir and the Ovenden Moor wind turbines (NE).

★ Just before reaching the summit we cross LIMERS' GATE (note the marker posts), a centuries old packhorse route used primarily for transporting lime from Worsthorne in Lancashire to farms in the Calder valley, where it was used to combat the acidity of the land.

THE NATIONAL TRUST
CRIMSWORTH DEAN

A memorial seat at LUMB BRIDGE is perfectly sited to provide an enchanting view of an idyllic beauty spot. Here Crimsworth Dean Beck rushes under an ancient, elegant packhorse bridge to plunge into a dark pool in a deep, tree-shaded ravine. The potential danger of allowing children free rein here will be evident. Beautiful, yes, but not a place for larking about. The valley is particularly rich in birdlife. Dippers and herons frequent the beck, sparrowhawks quarter the steep slopes in search of prey, whilst the woodlands provide excellent cover for such species as woodpeckers and long-tailed tits. Detour R at point ⑨ to inspect the ruins of NOOK, a once-prosperous 18th century farmhouse.

ABEL CROSS
is a special offer (2 for the price of 1). Legend has it that the twin shafts show where two lovelorn swains were interred after killing each other in a duel over a local farm wench. Less fanciful, but more likely, is that they were a) waymarks on a medieval packhorse route or b) monastic boundary markers.

Small ruined building, Sunny Bank

15 CLIVIGER GORGE

6 MILES

P Holme Chapel. Large layby on the A646 about ½ mile SE of the village. Grid ref: 880 279.

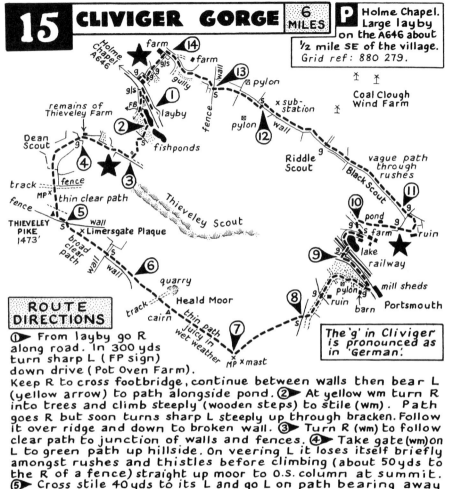

ROUTE DIRECTIONS

① From layby go R along road. In 300 yds turn sharp L (FP sign) down drive (Pot Oven Farm).
Keep R to cross footbridge, continue between walls then bear L (yellow arrow) to path alongside pond. ② At yellow wm turn R into trees and climb steeply (wooden steps) to stile (wm). Path goes R but soon turns sharp L steeply up through bracken. Follow it over ridge and down to broken wall. ③ Turn R (wm) to follow clear path to junction of walls and fences. ④ Take gate (wm) on L to green path up hillside. On veering L it loses itself briefly amongst rushes and thistles before climbing (about 50 yds to the R of a fence) straight up moor to O.S. column at summit.
⑤ Cross stile 40 yds to its L and go L on path bearing away from wall/fence. Through crosswall (wm) and forward with wall on R. ⑥ When wall begins to curve away R keep straight on (small cairn) along thin path. ⑦ Just before reaching a mast the path turns L (Burnley Way sign) and descends to stile (with yellow-topped post) in crosswall. ⑧ Turn L down broad track. Follow it past ruin and down to main road. Turn L up road. ⑨ Turn R (FP sign) through metal gate, cross railway and follow track round LH end of lake and up to farmyard. Here take gate or ladder-stile on L to green track up hillside. ⑩ A few steps beyond a gate turn sharp R up green path. At large ruin turn L (wm) and follow track curving L up to gate in crosswall (ignore an arrow pointing L). ⑪ Forward alongside wall on L. ⑫ Cross small ladder-stile (wm) and continue along LH side of wall. Follow marker-posts down to ladder-stile. ⑬ Pass to R of ruined walls then descend alongside gully on L. Go R along farm road. ⑭ At house turn L through small gate. Descend by wall to gate into wood, then down wallside path. At bottom turn R to road and follow it L back to car.

The 'g' in Cliviger is pronounced as in 'German'.

40

A HIGH-LEVEL CIRCUIT OF A DRAMATIC GORGE FAMOUS FOR ITS BIZARRE AND SPECTACULAR ROCK FORMATIONS. THE TOUGHEST WALK IN THIS BOOK, WITH STEEP CLIMBS ON EITHER SIDE OF THE VALLEY AND LOTS OF ROUGH, TUSSOCKY MOORLAND. IN FAIR WEATHER – AN EXHILARATING EXPEDITION WITH SUPERB AND EVER-CHANGING VIEWS. IN FOUL WEATHER – HIGHLY EXPOSED AND UNPLEASANT. IN MIST – DON'T EVEN THINK ABOUT IT. 4 SMALL LADDER-STILES (2 WITH ADJACENT GATES). ½ MILE ON MOTOR-ROADS (WITH WALKWAYS).

15

Eagle Rock, aka Beacon Rock.

★ CLIVIGER GORGE ★

Midway between Burnley and Todmorden the A646 enters a narrow, steep-sided valley, the most striking feature of which is the long line of shattered gritstone crags along its western flanks. These cliffs, known collectively as 'Thieveley Scout'(✱), give the hillside an astonishing 'crinkle-cut' appearance — a quite sensational and unforgettable sight.
✱ 'Scout' means 'high, overhanging rocks'.

The **FISHPONDS** at point ② were built by the Whitaker family in the early 19th C. In 1991 the ponds, which had become silted-up and choked with weed through almost a century of neglect, were restored to their original condition by the Todmorden Anglers' Society.

This prominent outcrop high on the slopes of Dean Scout is well-seen on the approach to point ④. The rock is in an unstable condition, and on no account should you attempt to stand on top of it, as the author is doing above. He should have more sense at his age.

THIEVELEY PIKE

← lost property

The summit is a drab and dreary place, adorned only by a rather grubby-looking O.S. column, a scruffy wire fence and, on the author's last visit, an old glove left behind by some careless wayfarer. Anything less like a 'pike' ('peaked top of a hill') is hard to imagine, but its saving grace is its excellence as a panoramic viewpoint. Pendle Hill, with its 'Big End', features prominently to the NW, with the Bowland Fells beyond. Close at hand to the N lie Black Hameldon and Boulsworth Hill, backed by the limestone hills of the Dales, including the instantly recognisable Ingleborough and Penyghent. Thieveley's western slopes, known as Deerplay Moor, drop gently into Rossendale.

THE BURNLEY WAY

a 40 miles long footpath, attains its highest point at the summit of Thieveley Pike.

B

COAL CLOUGH WIND FARM, on Warcock Hill, was one of the first wind farms to be established in Britain. Its 24 spectral turbines hideously deface the landscape.

PORTSMOUTH is said to have been named by an old sailor who settled in this neck of the woods long ago.

← BURNLEY 4¾ml
ROCHDALE 10m →

The Limersgate Plaque

16 HEPTONSTALL & COLDEN — 5 MILES

P Heptonstall. There are two car parks, one in the village centre and one at the S edge of the village. The walk is described as starting from Weavers Square, in the village centre. Grid ref : 986 281 Alternatively you could start at point ⑤ by using the N.T. car park at Clough Hole, on the Heptonstall – Widdop road. Grid ref : 987 292

ROUTE DIRECTIONS

① ► Start along Townfield Lane, which soon becomes a walled track. When wall on L ends go ½ L across two fields. ② ► Go L along road to stile (FP sign) on R. Forward to stile into wood, but DON'T USE IT. Instead turn L to follow clear path along edge of wood. ③ ► On reaching walled green track on L leave woodland path and take gap-stile in wall – corner (near a telegraph pole). Cross bottom of field to stile back onto woodland path, which soon begins to descend gently (ignore a stile on L). ④ ► Path meets broad track at hairpin bend. Follow it L up to road. ⑤ ► Go R along road and L up farm road (FP sign). Before farm bear L (FP sign) along green path. At guidepost go straight on up sunken path. ⑥ ► Pass to immediate R of house. At crosswall go L between walls (wm) to continue forward on clear path. ⑦ ► Cross stile and straight on up moor for 20yds, then turn L along broad path (Pennine Way). At farm it turns R to climb alongside wall on L. Keep close to this wall to go through gate and descend path between old walls. At tarmac lane go 10 paces R to fenced path (PW sign). ⑧ ► Cross road to farm road. At farmhouse turn L through gate/stile, pass into next field on R and head for a stile at its bottom LH corner. Descend walled path to junction and go R to view bridge. ⑨ ► Return to junction and continue up causeyed path. ⑩ ► Cross step-stile in wall-angle. At corner of next field causeyed path goes through stile and round wall-corner. ⑪ ► At path junction go L uphill, then R at another junction to pass L of house. At 4-way junction (with seat) go straight on down broad walled path. Stay alongside wall on L to join uphill tarmac lane. ⑫ ► Just before bend go R through gap in wall (FP Heptonstall) to path along top of wood. The path is waymarked and climbs over outcrops and boulders. Take care to avoid any paths descending R. ⑬ ► Turn L (wm) up walled path which leads back into Heptonstall.

MODERATE, WITH PLENTY OF UPS AND DOWNS BUT NO REALLY STEEP GRADIENTS. STARTING FROM A QUAINT, 'TIME-WARP' VILLAGE, THIS SUPERB SHORT WALK BOASTS A STRING OF HIGHLIGHTS INCLUDING BEAUTIFUL WOODLANDS, HEATHER-CARPETED MOORS, ANCIENT CAUSEYED PATHS AND A PICTURESQUE OLD PACKHORSE BRIDGE IN AN IDYLLIC SETTING. THE ABIDING MEMORIES OF THE WALK, HOWEVER, WILL BE THE THRILLING VIEWS DOWN FEARSOME DECLIVITIES INTO THE VALLEYS OF HEBDEN WATER AND COLDEN WATER. ACROPHOBICS MAY FEEL APPREHENSIVE ON THE BRINK OF THE SPECTACULAR PRECIPICE AT POINT ⑬. NO LADDER-STILES. MOTOR-ROAD WALKING NEGLIGIBLE. THE WOODLAND PATHS CAN BE MUDDY AND SLIPPERY.

16

HEPTONSTALL

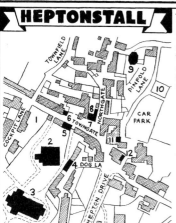

This ancient, higgledy-piggledy village is steeped in dramatic history. Heptonstall was once a prosperous handloom-weaving centre, more important than Hebden Bridge until the Industrial Revolution caused the textile industry to migrate to the valley floor. An hour or two's leisurely exploration among the tangle of buildings, soaking up the atmosphere of a bygone age, is an absolute MUST. The village plan and a few brief notes are all that space in this book will allow, but detailed guidebooks and leaflets are sold at the Post Office.

KEY TO PLAN: 1 WEAVERS SQUARE. Laid out in 1968 and designed as a 'museum of stone'. 2 OLD CHURCH. Dedicated to St. Thomas a'Becket, and dates partly from 13th C. Closed after storm damage in 1847 and is now just a shell. 3 NEW CHURCH. Built 1854 and dedicated to St. Thomas the Apostle. 4 OLD GRAMMAR SCHOOL. Endowed 1642, rebuilt 1771, closed 1889. Now a small museum. 5 CLOTH HALL. 16th C. 'Pieces' of cloth (a piece was 30 yds long) were brought by packhorse to be sold here. 6 WHITE LION INN. 7 CROSS INN. Built c1617. Formerly called Stocks Inn. 8 NEW HOUSE. Displays the delightful stone figures illustrated above. Inscribed 1736. 9 METHODIST CHAPEL. Octagonal. 1764. 3rd oldest Wesleyan chapel in world, and oldest to have been in continual use since its inauguration. 10 PINFOLD. Stray animals impounded here until owner paid a fine. Picnic area since 1980. 11 DUNGEON. Dates from 1824. A damp, dark cellar. 12 THE GREAT WELL. Was walled up for many years due to contamination of the water.

Hebble Hole Bridge

This ancient little packhorse bridge now conveys Pennine Way pilgrims across Colden Water. An ideal picnic spot.

LUMB BANK was the home of the poet Ted Hughes. Born at Mytholmroyd in 1930, Hughes was Poet Laureate from 1984 until his death in 1998.

The path between points ⑫ and ⑬ provides a highly spectacular finale. After a rough scramble over a jumble of boulders in EAVES WOOD, we emerge onto a rocky bluff with a sensational drop from our very feet to the village of Mytholm far below.

P Jerusalem Farm. From the A646 at Luddenden Foot take signposted road to Booth. Drive through village and immediately after a sharp, steep bend turn L along Jerusalem Lane. Jerusalem Farm (car park and toilets) is ½ mile on R.
Grid ref: 036 278

ROUTE DIRECTIONS

①► From gate/stile at bottom of car park descend to cross Wade Bridge. Take path rising slightly L to wall-corner. Keep to RH side of wall (ignore stile) then go L round wall-corner to small gate into enclosed rising path. **②►** At house (The Hullet) continue up tarmac lane. At junction go R and in 80yds turn L up steep, rough track. **③►** At top of rise turn R up grass and R again (cw sign) along farm road. Join tarmac lane and immediately take wooden stile on L. Follow cairned path. **④►** Go L up rough lane. When wall on L ends go L over stile and R up thin path. Join an old cart-track briefly, then climb corner of embankment and walk along top of dam. Cross cart-track to thin path in heather, over stile and along top of another dam. **⑤►** At end of dam (stile) continue up broad track. Follow it past Haighcote Barn and on up to a large ruin. **⑥►** In front of ruin go L through wall-gap and follow wall on L to gate into farmyard. Go R up rough track. When it bends R turn sharp L and follow wall on L. **⑦►** Pass in front of big wrought-iron gates then turn L (wm) alongside wall. When wall turns away L keep straight on along narrow moorland path with marker-posts. Beyond a large cairn the path descends through heather, finally veering R to a stile. **⑧►** Go L for a few paces then R (FP sign) past end of house. Bear slightly R down field to stile in crosswall, then straight on, descending steeply. **⑨►** At a small waymarked post turn R down clear path which zig-zags down to stile in front of house. **⑩►** Go R along lane. Pass through gatehouse and follow broad track for just over a mile. **⑪►** Immediately past entrance to Upper Mytholm turn L along path (wm) to descend, through a series of stiles, to Luddenden Brook. Cross footbridge and follow path downstream to Wade Bridge.

NOTE If Luddenden Brook is in full spate the riverside path may be impassable. You can avoid drowning by going straight ahead at point ⑪. Keep L at a fork.

wind farm (see Walk 12)
⑦
Withens Head Farm
Slade
⑥
FB
tiny ladder-stile
marker posts
Moorlands (ruin)
g/s Haighcote Barn
Warley Moor
cairn
⑤
Rocking Stone
Rocking Stone Flat
Haigh Cote Dam
good path
heather
Cold Edge Dams
cart track
FB
Leadbeater Dam
gatehouse
⑩
redundant stile
⑧
bog
CW
wall
Moorcock Inn
④
Low Bridge
⑨
gatehouse
CW = Calderdale Way
cairned path
FB
barn and stables
Catherine House
FP
farm
g
farm road
tarmac lane
FP
Heys Lane
③
FP
Spa Wood
②
g
Upper Saltonstall
FB
⑪
g
g/s
Wade Wood
Clough Hole
Wade Bridge
g/s
①
Jerusalem Farm

44

A SPLENDID WALK, WITH REMARKABLY CONTRASTING LANDSCAPES RANGING FROM A SHELTERED, WOODED VALLEY TO THE BARE, WINDSWEPT EXPANSES OF WARLEY MOOR. THERE IS A LONG, STEADY (STRENUOUS ON A HOT DAY) CLIMB AT THE OUTSET, FROM WADE BRIDGE TO POINT ③, AND THE DESCENT FROM THE MOOR IS STEEP IN ITS LATTER STAGES. ALL THE REST IS EASY-GOING, BUT BE PREPARED FOR SOME BOGGY BITS IN WET WEATHER. IN MIST YOU MAY NEED THE HELP OF A COMPASS IN NAVIGATING THE MOORLAND SECTION. 1 LADDER-STILE (PROBABLY THE SMALLEST YOU'LL EVER SEE). MOTOR-ROAD WALKING NEGLIGIBLE.

JERUSALEM FARM
Outdoor Activities Centre

LUDDENDEN DEAN

is one of the loveliest of Calderdale's many side-valleys. 'London Dean', as the locals pronounce it, has limited road access and, in consequence, a feeling of remoteness and an air of utter rural tranquillity. Oak, birch, beech, rowan, holly and hazel are some of the trees you are likely to see in the valley's magnificent deciduous woodland, and there is birdlife in abundance, particularly along the course of the brook. The stately grey heron is frequently seen here.

WADE BRIDGE

Dates from early 19th C, but rebuilt after severe flood damage in May 1989.

UPPER SALTONSTALL

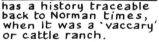

has a history traceable back to Norman times, when it was a 'vaccary' or cattle ranch.

The ruins at MOORLANDS suggest that this was once a farm of some distinction.

The two castellated GATEHOUSES encountered on this walk belonged to the CASTLE CARR ESTATE established by John Edwards, a Huddersfield wool merchant, in the mid-19th C. There was a huge and staggeringly ostentatious mansion, with extensive water gardens landscaped around a series of reservoirs. Edwards died in a train crash at Abergele in 1868, and successive owners found the estate too costly to maintain. The mansion was demolished in the 1960s.

CATHERINE HOUSE'S NAME MAY BE DERIVED FROM 'CATERAN' — A SCOTTISH RAIDER OR ROBBER.

The 'tiny ladder-stile'

18 CRAGG VALE

5 MILES

P Mytholmroyd. Car park by the main road (A646) just E of church and adjacent to White Lion pub. Grid ref: 014 260

ROUTE DIRECTIONS

①► Walk R along main road. At lights turn L over bridge and under railway bridge. At Shoulder of Mutton fork L (Sowerby 3). ②► Turn R up Hall Bank Lane. It bends L, then R, and climbs steadily. When lane turns L towards farm keep straight on up grassy path (SP Stake Lane). ③► Sharp R through gate/stile (FP Hollin Hey Bank). In 120yds fork L (wm) up hillside (clear path). Pass L of small barn and up wide track to gate/stile. ④► Don't use gate/stile. Bear R (wm) to follow path along top edge of wood. 100 yds beyond small seat path swings R down through wood, crossing a broad path to reach gate/stile at edge of wood. ⑤► Down walled path (causey), turn R between houses, follow drive down to motor-road and turn R. ⑥► At Spa Terrace turn sharp L down tarmac drive. Cross bridge and wall-stile on R to follow permissive beckside path to Clough Foot Bridge. ⑦► Go L up road for 30yds then R through gate/stile (FP Dauber Bridge). Path enters wood at a stile and soon curves L to cross footbridge. Up steps to a clear path slanting R up wooded bank. ⑧► At top turn L along farm road. Keep L at a fork (FP Erringden Moor). At junction go straight on up woodland path (FP Erringden Moor). ⑨► After a long climb go R over fence-stile and up to moor top. Forward past end of wall to level path alongside remains of old wall. ⑩► Just before reaching wall-corner fork L. Pass another wall-corner and descend diagonally (aim towards distant wooded valley) to stile (wm) in crossfence. Forward to descend alongside an old walled, sunken path. ⑪► Turn R along farm road. In 30yds take stile (wm) on L. Thin, clear path slants L down hillside, past pylon and down through woodland. ⑫► Cross farm road via two stiles. Descend, with stream on R, to slab bridge, then cross field to stile by large gate. ⑬► Go R down farm road. Turn L at farm and follow road down to Clog Mill. Cross main road and turn R along canal towpath. ⑭► At third bridge go up steps, turn R then L at junction.

CRAGG VALE IS A TRIBUTARY VALLEY OF CALDERDALE. THOUGH ONCE HEAVILY INDUSTRIALISED, IT IS A PLACE OF OUTSTANDING NATURAL BEAUTY.

46

ONE OF THE PRETTIEST WALKS IN THE BOOK, FEATURING A SERIES OF EXQUISITE WOODLAND PATHS WITH, FOR ADDED VARIETY, SHORT SECTIONS OF SHADY RIVERSIDE AND BREEZY MOOR TOP. THE WALK IS STRENUOUS, WITH TWO LONG CLIMBS BETWEEN POINTS ②-④ AND ⑧-⑨ AMOUNTING TO 1130' OF ASCENT, BUT THERE'S A NICE EASY ¾ MILE FINISH ALONG THE CANAL TOWPATH. ALTHOUGH ALMOST EXCLUSIVELY ON CLEAR PATHS, THE ROUTE HAS MANY TWISTS AND TURNS AND CLOSE ATTENTION SHOULD BE PAID TO THE ROUTE DIRECTIONS. NO LADDER-STILES. ⅓ MILE ON MOTOR-ROADS (NEARLY ALL WITH PAVEMENTS). ALLOW AT LEAST AN HOUR FOR A VISIT TO THE FASCINATING CLOG MILL.

18

MYTHOLMROYD

stands where the side-valley of Cragg Vale joins the Calder. The village is largely a product of the Industrial Revolution, and is very tightly squeezed into its narrow valley (if you walk N to S through Mytholmroyd you will cross canal, road, river and railway all within the space of 300 yds). As a tourist centre Mytholmroyd is completely overshadowed by its near neighbour Hebden Bridge, but the casual visitor will find much of interest here. Facing each other at the village centre are the handsome Victorian church of St. Michael and the Dusty Miller Inn, an 18th C. haunt of the infamous Cragg Vale Coiners.

Shoulder of Mutton, Mytholmroyd

David Hartley in York Gaol, as depicted in the Coiners Exhibition at the Clog Mill

THE CRAGG VALE COINERS
A STORY OF FRAUD, INTRIGUE, MURDER & REVENGE

The 'coiners' were a notorious gang of 18th C. counterfeiters led by David Hartley, who was known as 'King David'. Hartley, who was by all accounts a violent thug, lived at Bell House, a remote dwelling ¼ mile SE of point ⑨ of our walk (it can be viewed by a short detour L along the moor edge). The coiners obtained gold coins from local innkeepers, clipped off the milled edges, then re-milled them by pressing the soft gold onto a file. The coins were then returned to their owners with about half of the clipped gold. In 1769 the government appointed William Deighton to investigate, and in October of that year King David was arrested and taken to York Castle. On 10th November, around midnight, Deighton was brutally murdered. Several suspects, including one Matthew Normanton, were arrested, but all were acquitted. On 28th April 1770 David Hartley was hanged at Tyburn, near York. His grave can be seen near the old church at Heptonstall. Normanton was eventually re-arrested in 1775 on a charge of 'felonious assault'. Half-an-hour before he was hanged he confessed to the murder of Deighton. His body was hung in chains on Beacon Hill, Halifax, and remained there for several years. A somewhat gruesome 'Coiners Exhibition' can be seen at the Clog Mill.

WALKLEY'S CANALSIDE MILL, which has been making clogs and clog soles for over 130 years, has now developed into a major tourist attraction, with children's play areas, a tea shop, imaginative exhibitions & shops selling a quite astonishing variety of goods.

P Todmorden. Large car park in front of the Hare and Hounds pub at the junction of Burnley Road (A646) and Hunters Lane, ½ mile NW of town centre.

Grid ref: 930 250

ROUTE DIRECTIONS

①► From car park go R along main road and turn R along Stoney Royd Lane. Follow it as it passes under a huge railway arch, zig-zags up past Stannally Farm and climbs, with a wooded ravine on the L, to a gate. ②► Follow track to R. Pass L of farm, up walled track, and at junction go R along green lane. ③► At end of walled lane keep straight on through rushes and along a superb paved path. ④► Opposite farm turn sharp L through gateway and up cart-track. At top keep straight on up tarmac lane, passing a mast. ⑤► Turn L at road junction and at first sidewall cross stile (wm) on L to follow green path to O.S. column on Bride Stones. ⑥► Thin path heads towards wind farm. Follow it to farthest cluster of rocks, go R along cart-track and R up farm road. ⑦► Turn L along road (short detour R if you fancy a pint). ⑧► Turn L down Mount Lane then L along farm road (BW sign). Pass L of farm and keep straight ahead along walled track, which eventually crosses a stream and rises slightly. ⑨► At top of rise take gate/stile (wm) on R to wallside path. Stay with wall as it turns L down to gate/stile. Descend broad woodland track. ⑩► Immediately below first building turn sharp L along rough, walled lane. Cross top end of a street and go straight on along a private-looking drive. Before reaching the house at its end fork R into a narrow path between a hedge and a metal fence, to emerge at the railway arch on Stoney Royd Lane. Turn R to return to main road and car park.

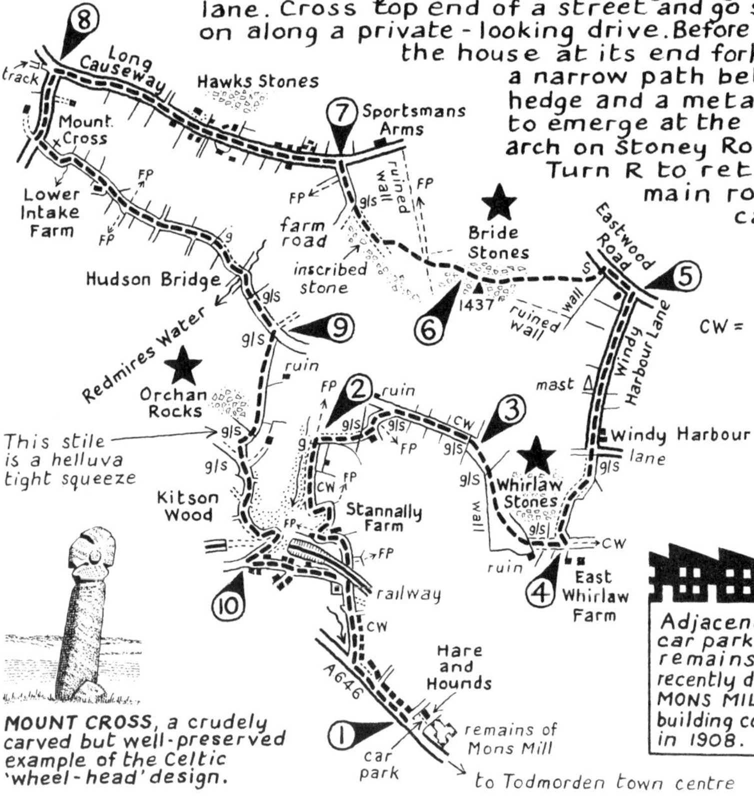

CW = Calderdale Way

This stile is a helluva tight squeeze

MOUNT CROSS, a crudely carved but well-preserved example of the Celtic 'wheel-head' design.

Adjacent to the car park are the remains of the recently demolished MONS MILL, a huge building constructed in 1908.

48

AN INTRIGUING TOUR OF THE VARIOUS WEIRD ROCK FORMATIONS ON THE STEEP HILLSIDES TO THE N. OF TODMORDEN. QUITE STRENUOUS - PARTICULARLY THE LONG CLIMB UP STONEY ROYD LANE TO POINT ②. THE SHORT SECTION FROM THE BRIDE STONES O.S. COL. TO THE 'INSCRIBED STONE' WOULD NEED CARE IN MIST; OTHERWISE GOOD, CLEAR PATHS AND TRACKS THROUGHOUT. FIRM GOING EXCEPT FOR THE WALLED TRACK BETWEEN LOWER INTAKE FARM AND POINT ⑨, WHICH CAN BE DECIDEDLY SQUELCHY. NO LADDER-STILES. 1¾ MILES ON QUIET MOTOR-ROADS.

HARE & HOUNDS

THE WHIRLAW STONES

A huge mound of heather-clad gritstone outcrops prominently in view from the streets of Todmorden and prominently featuring in regional folklore. Local author William Holt's novel 'The Wizard of Whirlaw' tells how the wizard's fierce daughter Jane, having fallen in love with a young weaver, Alan Haugh, attempts to lure him up from the valley by wandering nocturnally among these stones setting the heather alight. Our route passes below the Whirlaw Stones on a superb section of causeway.

THE BRIDE STONES

ARE AN EXTENSIVE GROUP OF WEATHERWORN ROCKS BENEATH AN OUTCROPPING FACE OF MILLSTONE GRIT, AND THE TRUE BRIDE STONE IS A QUITE ASTONISHING OBJECT – HUGE AND BALLOON-SHAPED, AND BALANCED PRECARIOUSLY ON A TINY, ERODED PEDESTAL. THE NEARBY O.S. COLUMN, AT 1437', MARKS THE HIGHEST POINT OF THE WALK.

Mrs. Author and the true Bride Stone.

𝔐ount 𝔆ross

is one of the finest crosses in the South Pennines. Opinions vary about its age, but it is thought to date back to early medieval times and was possibly a guidestone on a monastic route. Some claim that it is even older, and that it marks the spot where St. Paulinus preached in the 7th C. whilst escorting Princess Ethelberga of Kent to Northumbria to marry King Edwin.

★

THE SPORTSMANS ARMS was built on an old trading route known as **THE LONG CAUSEWAY**, and in bygone days it would cater for packhorse men and drovers. The pub is haunted by a ghost named Rebecca who calls in for a drink from time to time (they serve spirits).

The Sportsmans Arms

Half-way round the walk. Ideal for a lunch stop

P Gorpley Clough, on the A681 Todmorden - Bacup road, ¾ mile W of Gauxholme. Small, fenced parking area (for about 4 cars).
Grid ref: 918 236

to Bacup
small car park

to Todmorden

Gorpley Clough

Counting Hill

Range Hoyle

Gorpley Reservoir

old mine road
mine spoil
air shaft

Inchfield Moor

Inchfield Pasture

Foul Clough Road

Limers Gate
superbly built wall

pond

Limers Gate

Trough Edge End
1489'

old trough

pylon

pool

Pot Oven

Freeholds Top

mine

powerline

Coolam (ruin)

Ramsden Clough Reservoir

broad track

causeyed path

ROUTE DIRECTIONS

① Car park has two exit - stiles. Take LH one (as seen with your back to road). Good path, stepped in places, climbs wooded clough, via several footbridges, to swing - gate opposite Water Treatment Plant. Turn R along reservoir access road. ② At T - junction turn L up a rough track. On reaching a cattle - grid take stile (wm) on its R and climb with wall on L. When wall turns away L keep straight on, contouring hillside to join a cart - track at a gate/stile in cross - wall. ③ Follow cart-track, which soon ends at a gate. Don't use gate, but keep straight on alongside fence - cum - wall on L. ④ When wall turns down L go straight on. There's no path, but just below the skyline you'll see two patches of mine - spoil. Aim for the RH (larger) patch and continue beyond it up to ladder - stile in crosswall. ⑤ Don't cross ladder - stile. Turn L (SP Limers Gate) to follow wall. Ignore another Limers Gate sign. Stay on LH side of wall, then go L alongside fence and ruined wall. A gate gives access to O.S. column. ⑥ Head away from fence, bearing very slightly L (towards group of pylons on far skyline). Thin path soon drops steeply towards ruined farmhouse. Follow broad track (very stony at first) for about ¾ of a mile. ⑦ Look for small pool on L, and here turn L (SP Gauxholme) to follow clear path. It is causeyed in places and has marker - poles. At a wall - corner it joins a broader track coming in from the R. The track swings L to run alongside a wall on R. Eventually the track begins to descend steeply, and executes a hairpin bend as it drops to reach the main road at a mill (Stoneswood Mill). ⑧ Turn L and follow the road (pavement) for ¼ of a mile back to the car park.

A SHORT BUT FAIRLY STRENUOUS WALK OVER THE HIGHEST OF THE HILLS IN THE TODMORDEN AREA. THE FIRST ½ MILE, UP A WOODED RAVINE, IS A SHEER DELIGHT; THEREAFTER THE TERRAIN IS PREDOMINANTLY ROUGH MOORLAND – MUCH OF IT PATHLESS. THE CLIMB FROM POINT ④ TO THE RIDGE TOP IS QUITE A HARD SLOG. IT'S ONLY ABOUT 260′ OF ASCENT, BUT SEEMS CONSIDERABLY MORE. IN MIST THIS SECTION WILL REQUIRE THE USE OF A COMPASS, AS WILL ALSO THE DESCENT FROM POINT ⑥, AND THE WALK IS BEST AVOIDED IN SUCH CONDITIONS. IN CLEAR WEATHER ROUTE-FINDING SHOULD NOT BE A PROBLEM. NO LADDER-STILES. ¼ MILE ON A MOTOR-ROAD (WITH PAVEMENT).

20

In summer the general drabness of these peaty, acidic moors is relieved by great expanses of the fluffy white seeding heads of **COTTON-GRASS**, which, oddly enough, is not a grass at all, but belongs to the sedge family (Cyperaceae). The silky tufts consist of fine, brittle hairs which grow from the fruits and carry them for long distances in the wind. **COMMON COTTON-GRASS** (Eriophorum angustifolium) flowers May-June and has several nodding heads at the top of each stem. **HARE'S TAIL COTTON-GRASS** (E. vaginatum) flowers a little earlier (April-May) and has only a single upright head.

GORPLEY CLOUGH

Campion

A much-restored path up this beautiful little glen gets the walk off to an enchanting start, for the sylvan woodland and the sparkling beck, with its waterfalls, cascades and shady pools make this one of the prettiest places in this book. Campion, ragwort and wood anemone are but three of the many species of wild flowers which decorate the ravine, and the botanist will also be enthralled by the profusion of ferns. Make the most of Gorpley Clough, for you'll find yourself in a vastly different landscape all too soon.

Wood Anemone

THE RESERVOIRS

GORPLEY RESERVOIR, built to supply Todmorden, was completed in 1905 and has a surface area of 16 acres. The setting is quite dramatic, with the steep hills on its south side rising almost sheer out of its dark waters.

The smaller **RAMSDEN CLOUGH RESERVOIR** was also built to supply Todmorden, but shortly after its completion in 1888 it was sold to Rochdale Corporation.

★

The 'superbly built wall' on the ridge is the work of a master craftsman.

THE MOORS

INCHFIELD MOOR offers extensive views, as one would expect from the loftiest of Todmorden's encircling hills. To the west, nestling in the ROSSENDALE VALLEY, are the industrial towns of BACUP and RAWTENSTALL, and to their right (NW) PENDLE HILL's unmistakable profile can be seen through CLIVIGER GORGE. The panorama eastwards features the long escarpment rising to the ubiquitous STOODLEY PIKE monument, and the jagged ridge to the south-east is BLACKSTONE EDGE. The summit of Inchfield Moor is unusual in that the O.S. column overlooks a sizeable pond.

KEEP FIDO ON A LEAD DURING THE NESTING SEASON (APRIL-JUNE)

21 STOODLEY PIKE FROM LUMBUTTS 6¼ MILES

P Shepherd's Rest Public House (marked PH on OS map) about ¾ mile W of the village of Lumbutts. Small roadside parking space opposite pub. Grid ref : 945 231

ROUTE DIRECTIONS

① From car park take gate (FP sign) by information board to broad, rough path slanting leftwards up hillside. **②** Ignore a path forking more steeply R (just before small pool on L). Main path keeps L and climbs very gently up RH side of clough. It narrows as it rises, but is always clear. **③** Path swings L across head of clough, doubles back along its other side briefly, then swings R to head towards distant monument. The thin, clear path keeps fairly close to the steep escarpment on the L. **④** Path joins broad Pennine Way track coming in from R and descends to a crossroads of paths. Cross the causeyed path and keep straight on past a tall standing stone (Long Stoop) and up through old quarries. Follow broad, level track to monument. **⑤** Turn R (E) along a broad path heading towards a plantation. Cross wall-stile, go L over ladder-stile (PW sign) and descend broad path. **⑥** Almost at bottom of field turn L along broad, level path (London Road). Follow it for about 1¼ miles. **⑦** At wall-corner keep straight on along walled track. At road turn R and walk through village. **⑧** At lone house and cemetery turn L (CW sign) down walled causeyed path. **⑨** At its end, with Top Brink Inn on your L, cross to a steeply descending enclosed path (wm). At bottom turn R to follow road back to Shepherd's Rest.

The monument was built to commemorate the downfall of Napoleon, but has fallen down itself twice.

PW = Pennine Way
CW = Calderdale Way

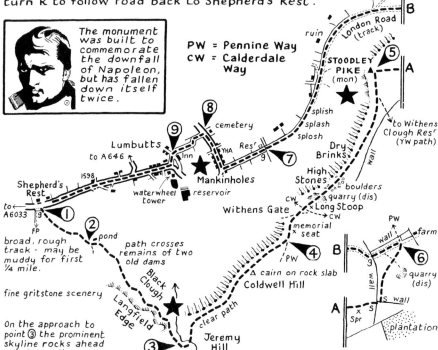

On the approach to point ③ the prominent skyline rocks ahead are Holder Stones

fine gritstone scenery

broad, rough track - may be muddy for first ¼ mile.

AN INVIGORATING WALK TO ONE OF THE REGION'S THREE MOST POPULAR OBJECTIVES (THE OTHER TWO BEING TOP WITHINS AND THE SUMMIT OF PENDLE). EASIER THAN IT LOOKS, WITH NO STEEP GRADIENTS. MUCH OF THE WALK IS IN FACT ON LEVEL GROUND, AND THE HARDEST BIT IS PROBABLY THE TRUDGE UP THE ROAD RIGHT AT THE END. GOOD, CLEAR PATHS THROUGHOUT, BUT THE HIGH-LEVEL SECTION, BETWEEN POINTS ③ AND ⑥, IS NOT MUCH FUN IN MIST. GENERALLY DRY AND FIRM UNDERFOOT, BUT THE LONDON ROAD TRACK CAN BE SLUTCHY* IN PLACES. I LADDER-STILE (QUITE A TALL ONE). I MILE ON QUIET MOTOR-ROADS. PACK A TORCH IF YOU INTEND TO CLIMB THE MONUMENT'S STAIRS.
* *Lancashire word meaning muddy, mucky, or something less polite.*

Shepherds Rest Inn, Lumbutts

The Shepherds Rest is the starting point, but don't use the pub car park without permission.

The memorial seat – a most unusual and pleasing design

STOODLEY PIKE

The enormous monument on Stoodley Pike dominates the Upper Calder valley and is the region's most famous and conspicuous landmark. Massively built of local millstone, it towers 120' above the moor and appears indestructable, but it has in fact twice collapsed. The original structure was a chimney-like obelisk erected in 1815 to commemorate the Peace of Ghent and the abdication of Napoleon. It is said that when workmen began to excavate the foundations they unearthed a number of human bones, which suggests that there may have been an ancient burial ground on the site. After being weakened by lightning, the monument fell down in 1854 at the outbreak of the Crimean War, and was rebuilt two years later when peace was declared. A further, partial, collapse occurred in 1918 on the day before the cessation of the Great War. There is an entrance on the monument's north side, above which is an inscription outlining its history, and a pitch-dark newel staircase winds up to a viewing balcony 40' above ground level.

Looking back to Stoodley Pike from the ladder-stile

MANKINHOLES

IS A SLEEPY PLACE NOW, BUT IN DAYS OF YORE WAS A BUSY HANDLOOM-WEAVING CENTRE. THAT THE VILLAGE WAS IMPORTANT DURING THE PACKHORSE ERA IS EVIDENCED BY THE LINE OF HUGE, ROADSIDE HORSE-TROUGHS. MOST VISITORS NOWADAYS ARE YOUTH HOSTELLERS, SOME OF THEM SEEKING RESPITE FROM THE RIGOURS OF THE PENNINE WAY. THE Y.H.A. BUILDING IS A FINE EXAMPLE OF A YEOMAN CLOTHIER'S HOUSE – ONE OF SEVERAL IN THE VILLAGE.

LUMBUTTS

IS DOMINATED BY A HUGE WATERWHEEL TOWER. THIS REMARKABLE STRUCTURE HOUSED 3 GREAT WHEELS 30' IN DIAMETER AND 6' WIDE. ARRANGED VERTICALLY, AND EACH WITH ITS OWN MILLPOND, THEY POWERED A COTTON-MILL.

22 STOODLEY PIKE

FROM WITHENS CLOUGH RESERVOIR

4¼ MILES

P Withens Clough Reservoir, reached by a narrow lane (Church Bank Lane) which leaves the B6138 at Cragg Vale (Grid ref: 001 232). If approaching from the south it is a very acute and awkward left turn - better to drive past it and re-approach from the other direction. The lane (beware potholes) ends at a small car park 300yds before the reservoir dam.

Grid ref: 987 232

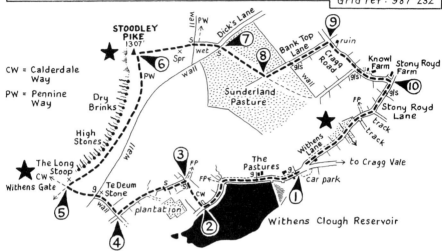

CW = Calderdale Way

PW = Pennine Way

ROUTE DIRECTIONS

① Go L up access road to dam. Continue forward along broad track, with the reservoir on your L. As track bears L, ignore a footpath sign (Stoodley Pike) on the R. ② Take next footpath on R (SP Calderdale Way) - a gently ascending green path. ③ At a wall-junction go L over stile (SP Calderdale Way) and forward with wall on R, soon using another stile to cross to the other side of the wall. Keep straight on, passing an old gateway and along a broad path. ④ At a crosswall don't use gate; turn R (SP Calderdale Way) up broad, wallside track. Through gate and straight ahead along broad path with marker-stones. Path soon becomes a stone causeway. ⑤ At a crossroads of paths turn R past a tall stone (Long Stoop). Clear path rises through an old quarry to follow the escarpment to the huge monument on Stoodley Pike. ⑥ Turn R (east) to follow broad track towards conifer plantation. Go through stile in crosswall, then ignore ladder-stile, keeping straight on with wall on L. ⑦ Take stile on R (FP Blaithroyd Lane) into plantation. Path runs along wide gap between two stands of trees. ⑧ Through gateway in wire crossfence and turn L (SP Yorkshire Water Permissive Path to Cragg Road). At a gate/stile path becomes a walled track (which can be awfully muddy). ⑨ At T-junction turn R (FP Cragg Vale) along another walled track. ⑩ At Stony Royd Farm go R down lane (initially tarmac) for a gentle descent leading directly to the car park.

> If you intend to climb the monument's interior staircase **REMEMBER TO PACK A TORCH**. It's pitch-dark and full of spiders – with maybe the odd dead sheep.

👣 ONE OF THE EASIEST WALKS IN THE BOOK, AND CERTAINLY THE EASIEST WAY TO THE TOP OF STOODLEY PIKE. STARTING AT 920', IT ENTAILS AN ASCENT OF LESS THAN 400' AND HAS NO STEEP GRADIENTS. BEING ENTIRELY ON CLEAR PATHS AND TRACKS, THE WALK IS SAFE IN MIST, BUT WOULD BE SCARCELY WORTH EVEN THE MODEST EFFORT INVOLVED IF YOU COULDN'T SAVOUR THE EXCELLENT VIEWS. NO LADDER-STILES. NO MOTOR-ROADS. IN WET WEATHER EXPECT SOME MUDDY SECTIONS BETWEEN POINTS ③-④ AND ⑥-⑨.

22

WITHENS CLOUGH RESERVOIR

Yorkshire Water

has a surface area of 60 acres and is capable of holding 293 million gallons of water. It was built between 1891 and 1894 for Morley Corporation, and supplied water to that town for 95 years, but now sends its water south-eastwards through the Manshead tunnel to Baitings Reservoir in the Ryburn Valley. Withens Clough is a lake of fitful moods. The wild setting of gritstone crags and bracken is particularly colourful when bathed in autumn sunshine; on a dark winter's day the reservoir can assume a forbidding — almost sinister — appearance.

The monument, Stoodley Pike

THE TE DEUM STONE

This squat, flat-topped stone is inscribed 'Te Deum Laudamus' (We Praise Thee O Lord). It was probably a resting-place for coffin-bearers carrying corpses from Cragg Vale for burial at Mankinholes.

☆ **WITHENS GATE** is a centuries-old packhorse route known also as the LONG CAUSEWAY (as are several other such routes in the region).The short section we tread on this walk has particularly well-preserved paving stones.
LONG STOOP is a stone pillar placed for the guidance of Withens Gate wayfarers. It is remarkably tall, and would look taller still were it not leaning at a drunken angle.

FOR SOME NOTES ON STOODLEY PIKE, PLEASE REFER TO WALK 21.

ON LEAVING THE MONUMENT LOOK OUT FOR THIS LITTLE STONE TROUGH COLLECTING COOL, CLEAR SPRING WATER. THE TROUGH WAS ONCE INSCRIBED 'PUBLIC SLAKETROUGH', BUT THE LETTERING IS NOW ILLEGIBLE.

🌲🌲🌲🌲
SUNDERLAND PASTURE PLANTATION is owned and managed by Yorkshire Water, and adds some scenic variety to the walk. Please remember that woodlands are very vulnerable in dry weather.

TAKE CARE
DO NOT START
FIRE

Todmorden - Littleborough road. Park on tarmac roadside verge in front of Bird i' th' Hand pub car park.

Grid ref : 944 201

ROUTE DIRECTIONS

1▶ Start along Warland Gate End (FP Pennine Way 1). Cross canal and follow road up between houses and round a hairpin bend. Stay on rising tarmac lane. **2▶** Lane turns R to buildings. Enter yard and turn L. Go through gate/stile (wm) then R through fence-gap and up to gate to R of house. Rough track rises to another gate, then climbs alongside stream to reservoir embankment. **3▶** For short cut go ½ L up steep path then L along top of embankment. For full walk go R up broad track. Cross footbridge over drain and follow path on low embankment between reservoirs. Path eventually swings L and heads through heather to far end of Warland Reservoir. **4▶** Cross concrete drain and go R along broad track. When drain turns R go L (wm) along a flagged path. **5▶** Pass along LH side of Gaddings Dam then bear L (wm) along thin path. **6▶** At crossroads of paths (cairn/marker post) turn L along clear path (Salter Rake) which soon becomes paved (old causeway). **7▶** At gate enter enclosed track. Join a drive, and when it forks keep L (straight on). **8▶** At next house (South Hollingworth) go through gate but ignore broad track rising L. Instead stay alongside wall on R (causeyed path). Pass L of next house (Dean Royd) and follow causeway. Cross small footbridge and rise to gate at Bottomley. **9▶** Forward between buildings. Turn R along tarmac lane, but in a few paces leave it in favour of a gate on R (wm). Descend enclosed cobbled path, cross canal bridge and turn L to follow towpath back to start.

Rake End

cairn/marker post

6

wall

Salter Rake Gate

Gaddings
MP. Dam

Basin Stone

ruined walls

Henshaw Wood

7

North Hollingworth

8

South Hollingworth

wall

FB

9

Dean Royd

Bottomley

summit railway tunnel

A6033

Stone House Bridge

Rochdale Canal

playing fields

A6033

WARLAND

Bird i' th' Hand

park here ➤

1

remains of former dam (Gaddings East)

Langfield Common

flagged path

wet moorland

PW drain

4

PW

short cut

Warland Reservoir

cairn/marker post   Rake End

Stony Edge

O.S. column ▲ Little Holder Stones

heather

Little Dove Lowe

Little Hazzles Reservoir

PW = Pennine Way

2 derelict farm

g/s

g/s

g/s

stream

3

PW

stream plunges underground

Light Hazzles Reservoir

THIS INTERESTING WALK HAS FOUR DISTINCT PHASES, VIZ:- 1) A 1 MILE CLIMB TO WARLAND RESERVOIR. 2) AN EASY 2½ MILE MOORLAND STROLL TO RAKE END. 3) A 1¼ MILE DESCENT, UTILIZING AN OLD PACKHORSE CAUSEWAY, TO THE CANAL. 4) A FINAL ¾ MILE SAUNTER ALONG THE TOWPATH. THE GOING IS GENERALLY GOOD TO FIRM, WITH THE PROBLEM OF A TRACT OF VERY SQUELCHY MOORLAND PRECEDING GADDINGS DAM HAVING BEEN SURMOUNTED BY THE LAYING OF AN EXCELLENT FLAGGED PATH. THE WALK IS NOT RECOMMENDED IN SEVERE WINTRY CONDITIONS, AND THE SHORT CUT AT POINT ③, WHICH SAVES ABOUT ½ MILE, SHOULD BE PREFERRED IN MIST. NO LADDER-STILES.

This row of cottages at Warland is dated 1655.

GADDINGS DAM

WAS ONCE ONE OF A PAIR. ITS FORMER COMPANION HAS BEEN EMPTY FOR MANY YEARS, BUT THE REMAINS OF ITS OLD EMBANKMENT CAN BE CLEARLY SEEN. A FREQUENT WINTER VISITOR TO THE DAM IS THE WHOOPER SWAN, WHICH DIFFERS FROM THE COMMON MUTE SWAN IN HAVING A BLACK, 'KNOBLESS' BILL WITH A YELLOW BASE. THE MUTE SWAN'S BILL IS ORANGE.

Mute Swan

Whooper Swan

THE RESERVOIRS

At the beginning of the 19th C. four reservoirs - Blackstone Edge, White Holme, Light Hazzles and Warland - were built on this moor, their purpose being to 'top-up' the water in the Rochdale Canal. By the 1920s, however, there was very little commercial traffic still using the canal, and in 1923 they were sold to Oldham and Rochdale Corporations and converted into supply reservoirs for East Lancashire's mill towns.

One of two tiny clapper bridges passed on the path 'round the back' of Warland Reservoir.

The **BASIN STONE** is a weirdly-shaped gritstone block just beyond Gaddings Dam and 35 yds L of the path. It probably owes its name to the two shallow, circular hollows in its top surface. It was used as a venue for Chartist * meetings in the 1830s.

* CHARTISM A radical democratic movement, mainly of the working classes, which flourished around 1838-50, and which derived its name from the People's Charter.

★ **SALTER RAKE**, its causeway stones well-worn through centuries of use, was part of an ancient packhorse route used primarily for transporting salt across the Pennines from Cheshire. Packhorse ways were the main routes by which goods travelled the country in the 18th C.

The **SUMMIT RAILWAY TUNNEL**, opened in 1840, is nearly 3,000 yards long and cost £250,000 to build. In 1984 this was the scene of a spectacular conflagration when a fuel train caught fire inside the tunnel.

24 GREAT MANSHEAD HILL 5¼ MILES

ROUTE DIRECTIONS

① Cross road to ladder-stile (SP Manshead Hill and Waterstalls Road), cross footbridge and climb alongside fence. Follow clear, waymarked path up to prominent cairn on skyline and on to O.S.

P Baitings Reservoir. Large layby on the A58 at the western tip of the reservoir, where two parallel power-lines cross the road.

Grid ref: 000 186

column. ② Continue forward along cairned path which eventually drops L to run alongside wall. ③ At crossroads of paths turn R along broad path passing to L of brick building (air raid shelter). At wall-corner cross stile (yellow arrow). Thin path heads for yellow-topped marker-post, then veers L. Cross fence-stile and keep straight on. ④ Turn R through metal gate and down track with wall on L. ⑤ At T-junction turn R along a tarmac lane. In 65 yds turn L (FP Blackshaw Clough) down rough lane. ⑥ Enter yard of house directly ahead. Turn R to pass round RH end of house, then take small gate (wm) on R and go L down walled, overgrown and sometimes muddy path. Cross stream and climb alongside wall on L. ⑦ At farm go through narrow gate (wm). Go straight on through farmyard and out along farm road. ⑧ At junction of tracks turn sharp R up grassy, walled track. ⑨ At next junction go R along tarmac road. Follow it, ignoring any side roads, for just over 1¼ miles back to the A58 and the layby.

'cairn on skyline'

Great Manshead Hill

wind shelter × / Manshead End 1368'
▲ O.S. column

cairn on skyline ▲ × memorial seat

Flints Hall

Greave Road (tarmac)

Blackshaw Clough

Great Greave

Far Slack

Blue Ball Road

BW seat

Clay Clough

former Blue Ball Inn

Blackhouse Reservoir (disused)

MP × wall
steep

FB ravine
Manshead

FB
A58
fence

pylon

A58 layby

Baitings Reservoir

TAKE CARE
DO NOT START
FIRE

The permissive path over Great Manshead Hill may be closed if there is a risk of fire.

NO DOGS

58

A WALK OF THREE DISTINCT PHASES. THE FIRST — AND BEST — SECTION IS AN INVIGORATING MARCH OVER WILD, LONELY MOORLAND. BETWEEN POINTS ③ AND ⑨ THE ROUTE FOLLOWS A SERIES OF FARM TRACKS AND OLD GREEN LANES THROUGH RATHER MORE HUMBLE SURROUNDINGS. THE CONCLUDING SECTION IS A LONG, LEISURELY STROLL DOWN A VIRTUALLY TRAFFIC-FREE ROAD. THE INITIAL CLIMB TO MANSHEAD END IS QUITE STEEP IN ITS UPPER STAGES; THEREAFTER THE GOING IS VERY EASY. THE LADDER-STILE AT THE OUTSET IS THE ONLY ONE ENCOUNTERED. THE WALK IS NOT RECOMMENDED IN POOR WEATHER.

24

THE PERMISSIVE PATH OVER MANSHEAD IS SUBJECT TO VARIOUS RESTRICTIONS. DOGS ARE NOT ALLOWED. NOR ARE MASS WALKS OR OTHER ORGANISED EVENTS. THE PATH MAY BE CLOSED IF THERE'S A FIRE RISK.

GREAT MANSHEAD HILL

Until recently Great Manshead had no paths and was out-of-bounds to walkers. In 1993, after much consultation, Calderdale's Countryside Service, with funding from Yorkshire Water, created a 2¼ mile-long permissive footpath along Manshead's fine ridge. A steepish climb up the nose of the hill brings you to a prominent cairn, and a nearby memorial seat is a comfortable place to digest both your jam butties and the panoramic view. You could also amuse yourself by counting the number of pylons visible - more than from any other point in this book. The true summit lies some 200 yds further along the ridge, and is marked by an O.S. column and a small wind-shelter.

This strange brick building, standing in the middle of a quarry and looking totally incongruous in its moorland setting, was a World War Two **AIR RAID SHELTER.**

GREAT GREAVE is a sturdy house of early 17th C. vintage. ★

BLACKHOUSE RESERVOIR, rendered surplus to requirements when Baitings was built, has stood empty for many years.

IN THE VICINITY OF POINT ④ YOU ARE LIKELY TO ENCOUNTER A SMALL HERD OF SHAGGY-COATED **HIGHLAND CATTLE,** THE HARDIEST OF ALL BRITISH BREEDS. DESPITE THEIR FEARSOME APPEARANCE THEY HAVE A REPUTATION FOR DOCILITY, BUT THE AUTHOR — CAUTIOUS AS EVER — WOULD ADVISE KEEPING A DISCREET DISTANCE. IF YOU GET ONE OF THOSE HORNS UP YOUR BACKSIDE YOU'LL KNOW ABOUT IT.

The **BLUE BALL** *was a 17th C. packhorse inn. Sadly it ceased trading in the late 1990s.*

Now converted into three houses.

BAITINGS RESERVOIR

was built between 1948 and 1956 on the site of a smaller reservoir. The massive concrete dam is over 500 yards long and holds back 775 million gallons of water. The reservoir has a maximum depth of 155 feet and a surface area of 64 acres.

P Blackstone Edge Reservoir. Large layby where the B6138 meets the A58 at the SE corner of the reservoir. *Grid ref: 974 180*

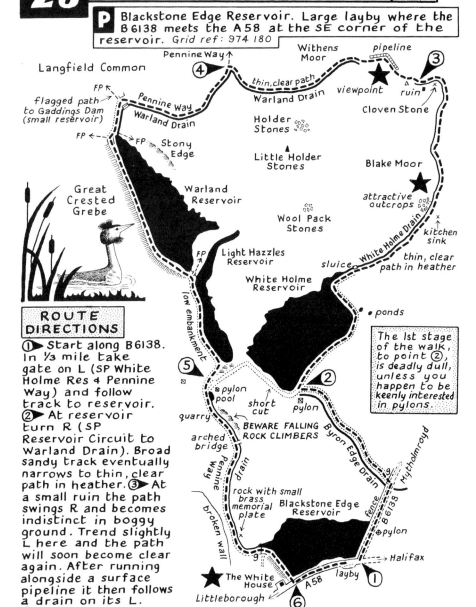

Pennine Way ↑
Withens Moor
pipeline
③

Langfield Common
④
thin, clear path
Warland Drain
viewpoint
ruin
Cloven Stone

FP ↖
flagged path to Gaddings Dam (small reservoir)
Pennine Way
Warland Drain
FP ←
FP ↗ Stony Edge

Holder Stones
Little Holder Stones

Blake Moor
attractive outcrops

Great Crested Grebe

Warland Reservoir

Wool Pack Stones

White Holme Drain
kitchen sink

FP ↑
Light Hazzles Reservoir
White Holme Reservoir
sluice
thin, clear path in heather

low embankment
⑤
pylon pool
short cut
②
pylon
• ponds

The 1st stage of the walk, to point ②, is deadly dull, unless you happen to be keenly interested in pylons.

quarry
arched bridge
BEWARE FALLING ROCK CLIMBERS
Byron Edge Drain
Mytholmroyd

Pennine Way
drain
broken wall
rock with small brass memorial plate
Blackstone Edge Reservoir
fence
B6138
pylon
Halifax

★ The White House
A58
layby
①
Littleborough ↙
⑥

ROUTE DIRECTIONS

①▶ Start along B6138. In ⅓ mile take gate on L (SP White Holme Res 4 Pennine Way) and follow track to reservoir. ②▶ At reservoir turn R (SP Reservoir Circuit to Warland Drain). Broad sandy track eventually narrows to thin, clear path in heather. ③▶ At a small ruin the path swings R and becomes indistinct in boggy ground. Trend slightly L here and the path will soon become clear again. After running alongside a surface pipeline it then follows a drain on its L. ④▶At junction turn L along broad Pennine Way track, still with drain on L. Track passes along RH side of first Warland Reservoir and then the slender Light Hazzles Reservoir. ⑤▶ Where track forks, near a pylon, keep R (straight on). ⑥▶ Go L along main road.

60

ONE OF THE LONGEST WALKS IN THE BOOK AND ONE OF THE EASIEST, FOR IT STARTS AT 1270' AND MAINTAINS ALMOST EXACTLY THE SAME HEIGHT THROUGHOUT ITS CIRCUIT OF A HEATHERY MOORLAND PLATEAU. THE MOST ATTRACTIVE SECTION IS THAT FROM JUST BEYOND WHITE HOLME RESERVOIR TO POINT ④, ALONG A THIN, CLEAR PATH WHICH IS ESPECIALLY DELECTABLE WHEN THE HEATHER'S IN BLOOM. THE REST OF THE WALK IS ON BROAD TRACKS AND RESERVOIR ACCESS ROADS WHICH ON A HOT DAY CAN BE A BIT HARD ON THE OLD PLATES OF MEAT. NO LADDER-STILES (IN FACT NO STILES AT ALL). JUST UNDER A MILE ON MOTOR-ROADS. THE B6138 IS FAIRLY QUIET AND THE BUSY A58 HAS A WALKWAY.

THE RESERVOIRS

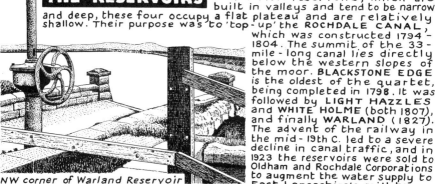

NW corner of Warland Reservoir

Unlike most reservoirs, which are built in valleys and tend to be narrow and deep, these four occupy a flat plateau and are relatively shallow. Their purpose was to 'top-up' the ROCHDALE CANAL, which was constructed 1794-1804. The summit of the 33-mile-long canal lies directly below the western slopes of the moor. BLACKSTONE EDGE is the oldest of the quartet, being completed in 1798. It was followed by LIGHT HAZZLES and WHITE HOLME (both 1807), and finally WARLAND (1827). The advent of the railway in the mid-19th C. led to a severe decline in canal traffic, and in 1923 the reservoirs were sold to Oldham and Rochdale Corporations to augment the water supply to East Lancashire's mill towns.

The many drains and ditches provide an ideal breeding habitat for DRAGONFLIES, which are particularly active in late summer. These striking and powerful insects are hunters and killers, overcoming their victims by out-flying them before delivering a few fatal bites.

Some interesting birds visit these waters – particularly White Holme, where great northern divers and great crested grebes are occasionally to be seen.

— * —

★ At the surface pipeline, just beyond point③, the path is scruffy and mutilated, but the star is awarded for the lovely view across Withens Clough Reservoir to the elegant Stoodley Pike monument.

The **WHITE HOUSE**, an old coaching and packman's inn, was originally called the Coach and Horses.

The small quarry near point ⑤, known as LIGHT HAZZLES EDGE, is a popular venue for rock climbers bent on developing the skills and techniques of their perilous pastime. There are some grotesquely-weathered outcrops here; note on top of one a boulder resembling a dog's head. Just beyond the quarry is a rather snazzy little stone bridge (illustrated).

26 BLACKSTONE EDGE 6¼ MILES

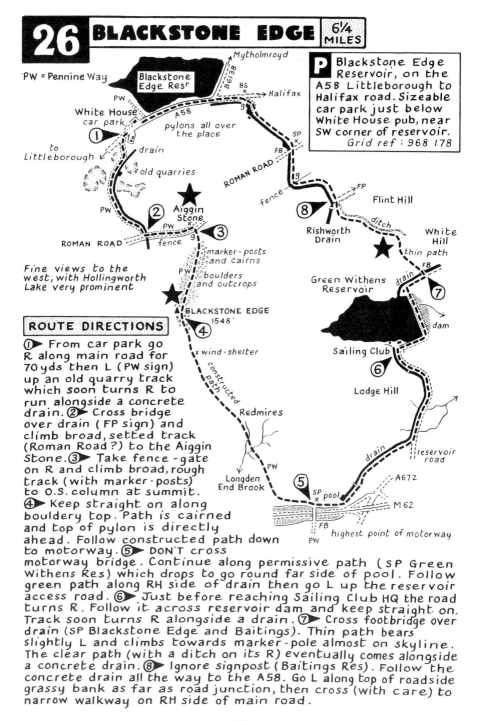

PW = Pennine Way

Mytholmroyd

Blackstone Edge Resr

White House car park ①

to Littleborough

A58

pylons all over the place

drain

old quarries

② Aiggin Stone

ROMAN ROAD

fence

③

marker-posts and cairns

Fine views to the west, with Hollingworth Lake very prominent

boulders and outcrops

★ BLACKSTONE EDGE 1548'

④

x wind-shelter

constructed path

Redmires

Longden End Brook

⑤

SP x pool

Halifax

BS

SP x

FB

ROMAN ROAD

19

fence

FP

Flint Hill

⑧

Rishworth Drain

ditch

White Hill

thin path

Green Withens Reservoir

drain

FB

⑦

dam

Sailing Club

⑥

Lodge Hill

drain

reservoir road

A672

M62

FB

highest point of motorway

PW

P Blackstone Edge Reservoir, on the A58 Littleborough to Halifax road. Sizeable car park just below White House pub, near SW corner of reservoir.
Grid ref: 968 178

ROUTE DIRECTIONS

① From car park go R along main road for 70 yds then L (PW sign) up an old quarry track which soon turns R to run alongside a concrete drain. ② Cross bridge over drain (FP sign) and climb broad, setted track (Roman Road?) to the Aiggin Stone. ③ Take fence-gate on R and climb broad, rough track (with marker-posts) to O.S. column at summit. ④ Keep straight on along bouldery top. Path is cairned and top of pylon is directly ahead. Follow constructed path down to motorway. ⑤ DON'T cross motorway bridge. Continue along permissive path (SP Green Withens Res) which drops to go round far side of pool. Follow green path along RH side of drain then go L up the reservoir access road. ⑥ Just before reaching Sailing Club HQ the road turns R. Follow it across reservoir dam and keep straight on. Track soon turns R alongside a drain. ⑦ Cross footbridge over drain (SP Blackstone Edge and Baitings). Thin path bears slightly L and climbs towards marker-pole almost on skyline. The clear path (with a ditch on its R) eventually comes alongside a concrete drain. ⑧ Ignore signpost (Baitings Res). Follow the concrete drain all the way to the A58. Go L along top of roadside grassy bank as far as road junction, then cross (with care) to narrow walkway on RH side of main road.

SURPRISINGLY EASY FOR A WALK WHICH INVOLVES TWO CROSSINGS OF THE MOORLAND 'TWIXT THE A58 AND THE M62. BLACKSTONE EDGE IS ONE OF ONLY FOUR SUMMITS IN THIS BOOK TO EXCEED 1500', BUT THE WALK STARTS AT 1250' AND ITS HIGHEST AND LOWEST POINTS DIFFER IN ALTITUDE BY ONLY ABOUT 350'. BEYOND THE SPLENDIDLY ROCKY SUMMIT THE SCENERY DETERIORATES IN QUALITY, BUT GOOD, FIRM, EASY-TO-FOLLOW TRACKS AND PATHS ALLOW ONE TO STRIDE OUT BRISKLY (SHOULD ONE SO DESIRE), AND THERE ARE NO STILES TO IMPEDE ONE'S PROGRESS. HALF-A-MILE ON A BUSY MOTOR-ROAD (WITH VERGES AND WALKWAYS). THE LANDSCAPE HERE HAS BEEN LARGELY FASHIONED BY THE HAND OF MAN, AS EVIDENCED BY THE QUARRIES, PAVED TRACKS, DRAINS, RESERVOIRS, ROADS AND, ABOVE ALL, THE MONSTROUS PYLONS.

26

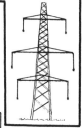

The wide, cobbled and flagged track which we tread between points ② and ③ is shown as ROMAN ROAD on the O.S. map, though whether or not this obviously ancient road was actually built by the Romans is a matter of some debate. It seems much too wide to be a paved packhorse track, and had it been a coaching or carters' road it would have not one but two lines of worn slabs along its length. Some opine that it was a 12thC route between a landowner's two estates in Elland and Rochdale, and was later used by packhorses (and by Daniel Defoe, who rode this way in the 1720s). Though remarkably well-preserved (*), the author was disappointed to note, on his last visit (17-6-02) that it was becoming overgrown and in need of an application of weedkiller.

(*) 'remarkably well-preserved' refers to the road, not the author).

Daniel Defoe 1660-1731

THE AIGGIN STONE
A MEDIAEVAL GUIDE STONE FOR TRAVELLERS
SOME 600 YEARS OLD
PLEASE RESPECT OUR HERITAGE
SUPPORTED BY LITTLEBOROUGH AND DISTRICT LIONS

The stone stands at the highest point of the 'Roman Road'. It has an inscribed cross, and also the date 1817 and the letter 'S' (for the district of Soyland), showing that it has been used as a boundary stone.

BLACKSTONE EDGE

is one of the very finest gritstone edges in the South Pennines. The summit O.S. column stands atop a gigantic boulder - an excellent coign of vantage from which to admire the superb panoramic view. To the W, beyond the prominent Hollingworth Lake, is the industrial plain of Greater Manchester. To the N lie Boulsworth Hill, Black Hameldon and Pendle Hill, which can be seen through Cliviger Gorge. E is Green Withens Reservoir and to the S are the high moors of the Dark Peak.

REDMIRES used to be one of the most obnoxious bits of the Pennine Way. Wainwright, in his 'Pennine Way Companion' (1967) describes it as a 'ghastly mess' and a 'filthy quagmire'. Fear not, however, for a good raised path has now been laid across it - dry as a bone and as simple as walking along a pavement.

THE DIVISION OF THE COUNTIES LANCASTER AND YORK SOYLAND DISTRICT

Old boundary stone - A58.

⁕ GREEN WITHENS RESERVOIR was built 1892-8 and was enlarged in 1925 to its present capacity of 298 million gallons.

27 WATERGROVE — 6 MILES

P Watergrove Reservoir. Drive through the village of Wardle (signed from the A58 Rochdale – Littleborough road) and continue up setted road to large car park below dam. *Grid ref: 911 176*

ROUTE DIRECTIONS

① Climb steps, go R along top of dam then L along broad track. ② Turn R (BW Shore ½ m) up cobbled track. ③ Through gate in 'castellated' wall and follow track R. ④ At a guidepost, where track veers L by an old wall, turn sharp L up clear path. ⑤ When path forks keep L. (Note the stone shelter on the skyline ahead. Our route goes below and well to the L of it). ⑥ Cross a bridleway (marker-post) and keep straight on (yellow arrow). Path descends L to small stream. ⑦ Cross stream and keep straight on (blue arrow) uphill on clear path. ⑧ At highest point of path turn L up rutted path to Rough Hill summit (cairn). Keep straight ahead along soggy path which drops to a slight depression. ⑨ Turn L here (towards distant Hollingworth Lake). Sketchy path soon swings R along a grassy groove, then drops to come alongside a broken wall. Follow fragmented line of wall towards a rushy col to R of heavily quarried Middle Hill. ⑩ At col turn L past old boundary stone inscribed with letter 'S'. Head for clump of trees (no continuous path). On nearing trees a clear path develops alongside a wall. Follow it, ignoring any paths rising R. ⑪ On reaching a broad track turn L (BW Watergrove ½ m). ⑫ At a marker-post turn R (blue arrow) down grassy path. In 30yds fork L along a less-obvious path (easily missed). Path becomes cobbled as it drops through a gully to a fence-stile. Cross foot-bridge, climb steps and go L up broad track. ⑬ At T-junction go R along broad track. Just before reaching reservoir it turns L (wm) to join outward route at point ②.
(A path 'inside' the reservoir wall provides a pleasant alternative)

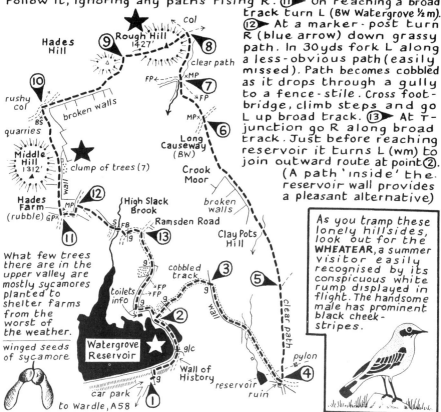

What few trees there are in the upper valley are mostly sycamores planted to shelter farms from the worst of the weather.

winged seeds of sycamore

As you tramp these lonely hillsides, look out for the **WHEATEAR**, a summer visitor easily recognised by its conspicuous white rump displayed in flight. The handsome male has prominent black cheek-stripes.

64

27

MODERATELY STRENUOUS. THE TRACKS AND PATHS ARE GENERALLY QUITE DRY AND THERE ARE NO STEEP GRADIENTS, BUT THERE'S A VERY LONG CLIMB (NEARLY 2 MILES) FROM POINT ④ TO THE SUMMIT OF ROUGH HILL. THERE BEING NO VESTIGE OF SHELTER FROM THE ELEMENTS, THE WALK CANNOT BE RECOMMENDED IN POOR WEATHER; **IN MIST IT IS POTENTIALLY DANGEROUS.** THERE IS ONLY 1 STILE (A LOW, WOODEN ONE) AND THE ENTIRE WALK IS ACCOMPLISHED WITHOUT SETTING FOOT ON TARMAC, THOUGH SOME OF THE TRACKS ARE SETTED OR COBBLED.

VILLAGE — WATERGROVE — RESERVOIR

Watergrove village, high in the valley above Wardle, developed over many years by utilizing its various natural resources. Coal was mined to provide heat and steam power, gritstone for building was quarried from the hillsides and the grassy slopes of the upper valley were ideal for sheep-grazing. At the time of its demise the village had over 40 houses, 2 pubs, a chapel, a smithy, 2 mills and a population in excess of 200.

The depression of the 1930s brought hard times to Lancashire in general and the cotton industry in particular. In the Rochdale area the local authority decided to put unemployed men to work on the construction of a new reservoir. Completed in 1938, Watergrove Reservoir (area 96 acres, maximum depth 87') had taken 8 years to build and the old village was submerged beneath 270 million gallons of water.

THE WALL OF HISTORY

Set into the reservoir wall at its SE corner are various datestones, window mullions and other artefacts. These were rescued from the drowned village and from the demolished farmsteads whose ruins still dot the valley above the reservoir. A few of the many datestones (the oldest of which is 1646) are illustrated below.

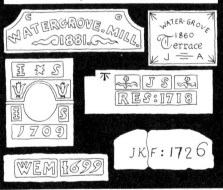

WATERGROVE MILL. 1881.

WATER-GROVE 1860 Terrace J ⟨==⟩ A

I ☆ S

E S

J 709

JS

RES:1718

WEM 1699

JK F:1726

summit cairn — Rough Hill

The summit of ROUGH HILL merits a star on the map merely by virtue of being the highest point of the walk. In truth 'tis a pretty dreary place, marked only by a modest, untidy cairn. Linger here for only as long as it takes to admire the pleasing view of Calderdale, with the Stoodley Pike monument prominent (as it is on so many of these walks). Note, to its right, the trio of reservoirs high on Walsden Moor (L-R Warland, Light Hazzles and Whiteholm), then sally forth rejoicing (it's all downhill now) along the soggy path to the west.

This old boundary stone pinpoints the start of the route of descent from the rushy col below Middle Hill.

WATERGROVE MILL was built in the late 18th C. and originally powered by water from Wardle Brook. The cotton-spinning mill later became steam powered, and was rebuilt in 1880 following a disastrous fire. The site of the mill is now occupied by a Sailboard Club HQ. There are public toilets at the rear of the building.

28 HOLLINGWORTH LAKE 4½ MILES

P Hollingworth Lake Visitor Centre. Pay and Display car park.
Grid ref: 939 152

KEY TO MAP
A site of Schofield Hall
B Higher Abbots
C Lower Abbots
D Antioch
E former Lodge Inn
F The Promontory
G TS Palatine
H Millers
I Fishermans Inn

ROUTE DIRECTIONS

① Walk up to lakeside road and go L along it. ② At end of embankment fork L (wm) up rough lane. Follow it through Hollingworth Fold (hamlet) and on to Syke Farm. ③ Straight on over the little 'cartwheel' bridge and up rough track (wm). Track runs roughly parallel with wall about 50yds to R. Ignore any paths branching L. ④ At wall-junction and gate with 'NO ENTRY' sign turn SHARP L to a path doubling back up hillside. At a junction of several paths turn sharp R to head back towards the wall you've just left. The clear path swings L to join a broad track. Go R along it, following pylon line. Pass to L of farm and on above M62 (don't cross it). ⑤ Go through gateway at end of fence and turn R (wm) to wall-stile. Follow top of low escarpment, then descend to pass through a gap in a broken wall (wm). You should now have an old wall and a gully on your L. Follow this shallow gully as it swings L to reach the site of Schofield Hall and two houses. ⑥ Opposite second house take fence-stile (wm) on R and descend steep field to stile/gate at its far LH corner. Climb hill beyond (clear path) to Higher Abbots. ⑦ Go L down access road and sharp R along tarmac lane. ⑧ Turn L (FP sign) over brick bridge and follow tarmac drive along lake edge. Continue on track around the wooded Promontory. ⑨ At start of embankment take gate/stile on L. Clear path eventually swings R by wall to iron ladder-stile. ⑩ Forward with wall and copse on R, then go R along farm road. ⑪ Enter farmyard and immediately past house turn R through small archway to gravel path. Turn L along lakeside track. ⑫ Turn R along Lake Bank and follow road around lake and back to Visitor Centre.

TWO ALTERNATIVES As the route is almost a figure-of-eight, it can be done as two separate short strolls by using the tarmac lane between points ② and ⑧. A - Visitor Centre - Syke - M62 - Visitor Centre (3 miles) or B - Visitor Centre - Promontory - Shaw Moss - Visitor Centre (2½ miles). Walk B can be further reduced by keeping to the lakeside path at point ⑨ and omitting the Shaw Moss section.

28

A SHORT AND VERY EASY WALK OFFERING A QUITE REMARKABLE DIVERSITY OF TERRAIN - TARMAC LANES, FARM ROADS, LAKESIDE PATHS, MOORLAND TRACKS, PATHLESS PASTURES AND A MINIATURE 'GOLDEN MILE' AND PROMENADE. GENERALLY FIRM UNDERFOOT, BUT THE SHORT SECTION BETWEEN THE M62 AND SCHOFIELD HALL CAN BE VERY MUDDY AFTER RAIN. 1 LADDER-STILE. ⅓ MILE ON A MOTOR-ROAD (WITH PAVEMENTS).

T' WEIGHVERS' SAYPORT

LAKE HOTEL

Great Crested Grebe

HOLLINGWORTH LAKE was built to supply water to the Rochdale Canal. It is a huge reservoir, with a surface area of well over 100 acres and a capacity of 475 million gallons even though it is nowhere more than 25' deep. Completed in 1798, the lake very soon became a popular visitor attraction, and several hotels were established around its shores to cater for the vast crowds which flocked here from local mill towns to enjoy sailing, fishing, swimming, drinking and general holiday revelry. A paddle-steamer plied the lake, ferrying passengers to and from The Promontory, where stood the Lake Hotel. In its Victorian heyday there were pleasure gardens here, and platforms for open-air dancing in the woods. Today there are picnic areas and toilets, and the rhododendrons remain, but the hotel has gone - replaced by a modern pavilion serving light refreshments. Hollingworth Lake was once known as 'T' Weighvers' Sayport' (The Weavers' Seaport), and the place still has an undeniable feel of the seaside about it. Lake Bank, with its fish and chip shops, ice-cream parlours, gift shops and amusement arcades, resembles a seafront, and the effect is enhanced by the kind of iron 'promenade' rails so often seen at coastal resorts. The area became a Country Park in 1974, and parts of the shore are now Nature Reserves. The Visitor Centre (opened 1977, extended 1985) is open all the year round, has a cafeteria and toilets, and offers a wide range of books, cards, leaflets and miscellaneous souvenirs.

HOLLINGWORTH FOLD

is a hamlet with buildings dating back more than 250 years. The large house on the right was a Victorian school and chapel. A footpath on its R runs behind the houses to a church built largely of corrugated iron and thus known as the 'Iron Church'.

The Iron Church

☆ **SCHOFIELD HALL** WAS BUILT IN THE 16TH C. AND OWNED BY THE SAME FAMILY FOR OVER 400 YEARS. IN ITS HEYDAY IT WAS ONE OF THE MOST STRIKING HOUSES IN THE DISTRICT.

SYKE FARM dates from 1758. Coal was once mined on the surrounding hillsides.

The **RAKEWOOD VIADUCT**, one of the biggest on the M62, has 20 massive, steel-reinforced concrete pillars rising to 140' above the valley floor.

This old van has reached its final resting place in a field near the M62.

29 SCAMMONDEN WATER | 5 MILES

P Moselden Lane, which leaves the A672 300yds NE of the Booth Wood Reservoir dam. ⅓ mile along the lane, on the L, is a car park and information board. Grid ref: 035 167

NOTE : In wintry conditions Moselden Lane may be unmotorable. In this case use the car park by the A672 near the dam (see map).

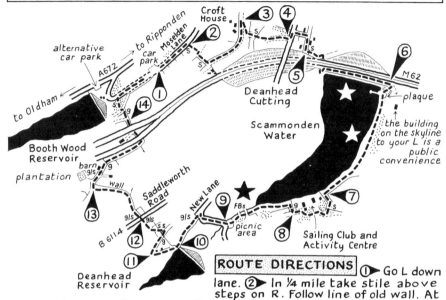

ROUTE DIRECTIONS ①► Go L down lane. ②► In ¼ mile take stile above steps on R. Follow line of old wall. At crossbank go R a few yards, then continue forward along LH side of fence on bank to stile. Go L along farm road. ③► Just past farmhouse turn very sharp R on path rising to cross bridge over drain, then slanting R up to ladder-stile into picnic area/car park. Cross it to its road entrance. ④► Go L along road for 30yds, R down walled path and R along road. ⑤► At road end take stile on L and descend to tunnel under M62. Follow path along top of dam. ⑥► At end of dam turn R to drop steeply to a 'circle' at lake edge. Follow lakeside path. ⑦► At Sailing Club turn L (FP sign) up path by trees. Cross stile and go R along track, then L along path towards plantations. It crosses a footbridge then drops to a large building on your R. Turn L here. ⑧► Turn R through metal gate (wm Kirklees Way) and descend to go L along lakeside path. Continue alongside feeder stream, ignoring two footbridges. ⑨► At picnic area cross stream and climb lane. At RH bend turn L to gate/stile and follow track to dam. ⑩► Don't cross dam. Climb concrete-topped wall (no stile) and follow wall on R. Keep below wall (don't go through gap) to pass two ruins. ⑪► Just beyond second ruin path hairpins R to ascend RH of two sunken ways. At top of rise take stile (wm) on L and go up sunken path to another. Cross ruined wall and bear R to gate/stile. ⑫► Cross road to gate/stile and follow fence, then wall, on R. ⑬► Approaching gap in crosswall turn R through old gateway and descend to pass to R of barn. Track swings R through gate, then passes under M62. ⑭► When track turns L keep straight on down by fence to kissing-gate. Go L along track for 5yds then turn R (wm) to path down wood to stile. Turn R to follow lane back to start.

UNDULATING, VARIED TERRAIN. GENERALLY FAIRLY EASY GOING, BUT BOGGY IN PLACES AND WITH SOME ROUGH GROUND IN THE VICINITY OF DEANHEAD RESERVOIR. THE WALK IS INTERESTING RATHER THAN BEAUTIFUL, ALTHOUGH THE SECTION ALONGSIDE SCAMMONDEN WATER AND ITS FEEDER STREAM (BLACK BURNE BROOK) IS A SHEER DELIGHT. FOR MUCH OF THE WALK YOUR EARS WILL BE ASSAILED BY THE NOISE OF MOTORWAY TRAFFIC, RANGING FROM A HUM TO A DRONE TO A ROAR DEPENDING ON ITS PROXIMITY. I LADDER-STILE. ½ MILE ON VERY QUIET MOTOR - ROADS.

WARNING AN OBSTACLE IS ENCOUNTERED AT POINT ⑩, WHERE ONE IS REQUIRED TO SCRAMBLE INELEGANTLY OVER A FAIRLY HIGH WALL. REASONABLY AGILE WALKERS SHOULD NOT FIND THIS MUCH OF A PROBLEM, BUT STIFF - JOINTED, SHORT-LEGGED INDIVIDUALS CERTAINLY WILL. THIS IS A PUBLIC RIGHT-OF-WAY, AND THE ABSENCE OF A STILE OR GATE HERE IS QUITE ASTONISHING.

DEANHEAD CUTTING

Here we can see how much hillside was cut away during motorway construction, the natural line of the hill being where the B6114 now runs on its bridge 120' above the M62. This magnificent bridge has a single span of 410'. Earth from the cutting was used to construct the dam.

SCAMMONDEN WATER

was one of the last Pennine reservoirs to be built, and is a truly remarkable feat of engineering. Survey and planning work began as long ago as 1962, but it was not until 14 October 1971 that Scammonden was officially opened by The Queen - an event commemorated

by a plaque near its NE corner. The huge reservoir had taken 3 years to build and a further 2 years to fill, during which process a dozen farms were consigned to a watery grave. From the outset Scammonden had been designed to allow public access to its shores, and between 1971 and 1975 over 100,000 trees were planted to enhance its beauty. What we now see is one of the country's most spectacular reservoirs, with hugely impressive vital statistics. It is almost a mile long and holds 1,730 million gallons of water, whilst its mighty dam - the biggest earth-filled dam in Europe - is 1050' long and carries trans-Pennine traffic on a motorway 249' above the valley floor.

STOTT HALL FARM engendered nationwide publicity in the 1970s as a result of the farmer's vehement protests against the building of the motorway. His dogged refusal to vacate his home led - incredibly - to the M62 being here split into separate carriageways, leaving Stott Hall stranded in the middle as, surely, Britain's noisiest farm.

BOOTH WOOD RESERVOIR was officially opened on 7th July 1971. Its colossal dam, 1,160 feet long and seen in awe-inspiring close-up on this walk, holds back 800 million gallons of water. The reservoir has an area of 54 acres and reaches a depth of 152 feet.

DEANHEAD RESERVOIR WAS COMPLETED IN 1872. IT HAS A SURFACE AREA OF 17 ACRES AND HOLDS 96 MILLION GALLONS OF WATER.

30 OXYGRAINS 5 MILES

P Oxygrains Bridge, on the A672 one mile NE of its intersection with the M62 (Junction 22). Small layby on E side of bridge. Grid ref: 004 159. There are several other nearby parking spaces.

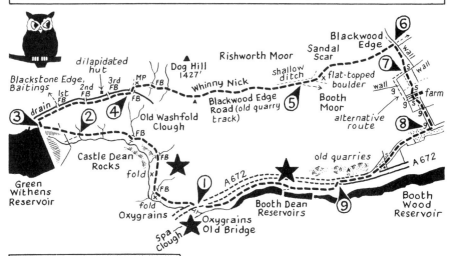

ROUTE DIRECTIONS

①► From layby cross road and follow excellent green path (SP Blackstone Edge, Green Withens Res) into ravine. Above Castle Dean Rocks the path swings L to remain parallel with stream on L. **②►** At a tiny side-stream, with a crosswall just ahead, the path forks. Go R, uphill. Path crosses broken wall and climbs to RH end of reservoir dam. **③►** Turn R along broad track, then R again to follow a drain. The drain is crossed by a series of footbridges. Ignore the first three. **④►** Cross 4th footbridge to path slanting R up hillside past marker-post. The thin, clear path across the moor is marked by posts and cairns. **⑤►** Ignore path forking R. Follow cairned path, which now has a shallow ditch on its L. At a flat-topped boulder the path veers L past a marker-post, then swings R along N side of ridge, heading for ladder-stile in distant crosswall. **⑥►** Don't cross ladder-stile. Turn R along wallside path, which soon bears slightly R to reach step-stile in crosswall. **⑦►** Cross this stile if you can (it's high and awkward – hellish awkward with a dog) and descend to ladder-stile at RH side of farm. ALTERNATIVE (to avoid doing yourself a mischief) Turn R alongside wall and round wall-corner to gate. Descend to gate in wall on L and forward to the ladder-stile. Go down farm access road. **⑧►** Where farm road turns L go R through swing-gate to cart-track through conifers. Follow it down to main road (en route you'll encounter another awkward stile. Its adjacent gate will probably be padlocked). Walk R along main road. **⑨►** 25yds beyond end of wall on L go L (SP Oxygrains, Green Withens) down grassy track. Follow it, keeping high above reservoirs, back to starting-point.

Except for the section between points ⑥ and ⑨, all the paths used on this walk are permissive (negotiated 1984-5 by Calderdale Countryside Service).

AN IDEAL SHORT STROLL FOR A BALMY SUMMER'S EVENING. EASY WALKING, MUCH OF IT LEVEL, OVER TYPICAL SOUTH PENNINE MOORS. IN CLEAR WEATHER THERE SHOULD BE NO ROUTE-FINDING HASSLE, THE THIN PATH BETWEEN POINTS ④ AND ⑥ BEING LIBERALLY FURNISHED WITH MARKER-POSTS AND CAIRNS, BUT IN MIST OR SNOW FIND SOMETHING ELSE TO DO. DOG-WALKERS SHOULD NOTE THAT THERE ARE TWO AWKWARD WALL-STILES; THE FIRST CAN BE BYPASSED BUT THE SECOND PROBABLY CAN'T. 300 YARDS ALONG THE BUSY A672, OTHERWISE NO TARMAC.

30

SSSI

These lonely moors are now officially designated as SITES OF SPECIAL SCIENTIFIC INTEREST. The wild landscape of heather, cotton-grass, bilberry and crowberry may seem harsh and inhospitable, but various attractive and uncommon birds find it to their liking and thrive here. Merlins, golden plovers, ring ouzels, lapwings and short-eared owls are just a few of the many species which regard these uplands as an ideal habitat.

lapwing

Bilberry aka blaeberry, whortleberry and blackheart. If picking to eat, take care not to confuse with sheep droppings.

THE RESERVOIRS

GREEN WITHENS RESERVOIR, a remote sheet of water in a stark moorland setting, is the HQ of a sailing club, and the normally sombre scene is sometimes considerably brightened by the colourful sails of the yachts. The reservoir was built 1892-8 and enlarged in 1925 to its present capacity of 298 million gallons. The two slender and attractive BOOTH DEAN RESERVOIRS were completed in 1923, but proved utterly inadequate for the available catchment area, and thus the huge BOOTH WOOD RESERVOIR was constructed. It is the area's newest reservoir (completed 1971) and, with a maximum depth of 152', has a staggering capacity of 800 million gallons. All these reservoirs were originally built to supply the Wakefield area.

cairn, Whinny Nick

Dilapidated hut by 3rd footbridge

Oxygrains Old Bridge

This lovely packhorse bridge now lies in the shadow of an ugly modern road bridge.

The QUARRIES at point ⑨ provided stone to build the Green Withens dam. The first and last stages of our walk follow the line of a 3½' gauge railway which carried the stone up to the site.

THE M62 MOTORWAY is in view for most of this walk and within earshot for all of it. This great engineering achievement of the 1970s is Britain's highest motorway, reaching a maximum altitude of 1220' at Windy Hill, just a couple of miles west of Oxygrains Bridge. The huge and graceful bridge which can be seen spanning the motorway away to the east is Deanhead Bridge (for illustration and details see Walk 29).

THE WALKS - A PERSONAL RECORD

Nº	DATE	TIME Start	TIME Finish	NOTES (Weather, Companions, Highlights, Disasters etc.)	Marks out of 10
1					
2					
3					
4					
5					
6					
7					
8					
9					
10					
11					
12					
13					
14					
15					